Matt Brough's delightful book, *Let God Send* offers a biblically sound approach to God's call and our response in discipleship and ministry in the world. Filled with personal anecdotes, reflections on ministry, and practical theology, this book will prove helpful to all who seek their life's calling.

— GRACE JI-SUN KIM, PROFESSOR OF THEOLOGY AT EARLHAM SCHOOL OF THEOLOGY AND AUTHOR OF SEVERAL BOOKS, MOST RECENTLY, *HOPE IN DISARRAY* AND *EMBRACING THE OTHER.*

Sending and being sent are significant and frequent themes in Scripture. Tracing the life of Abraham, Gideon, the disciples of Jesus, and other biblical figures, Matt reminds us that God's call still extends to us today. Equipped with authority and the promise of God's presence, being sent is not just what we do; it's also who we are. This book offers clarity, challenge, encouragement, and – maybe best of all – the permission to accept God's divine call on our lives to go.

— J.R. BRIGGS, AUTHOR OF *THE SACRED OVERLAP*, FOUNDER OF KAIROS PARTNERSHIPS (WWW.KAIROSPARTNERSHIPS.ORG)

Brough will guide you through the invitation every one of us has to join God's work in the world. God sends and commissions us all and gives us authority in the name of Jesus no matter who we are, what we've done, or what has been done to us. *Let God Send* is the perfect companion for those who are ready to cross whatever boundaries are necessary to make a move led by God's Spirit.

> — STEPHANIE WILLIAMS O'BRIEN, AUTHOR OF *STAY CURIOUS* AND *MAKE A MOVE*

Matt Brough reminds us that one cannot be a disciple of Jesus without embracing becoming an apostle as well. Christendom tried to push apostleship to the rear view. Brough, in Let God Send, is an essential voice in helping us all to bring it back to the front.

> — NICK WARNES, EXECUTIVE DIRECTOR OF CYCLICAL INC. AND CO-AUTHOR OF *STARTING MISSIONAL CHURCHES*

In an era of confusion and chaos such as we now find ourselves, voices like Matt Brough are needed more than ever. He is committed to fostering incisive conversations on spirituality that are accessible to almost anyone. You should listen to what he has to say.

— JONATHAN MERRITT, CONTRIBUTING WRITER FOR *THE ATLANTIC* AND AUTHOR OF *LEARNING TO SPEAK GOD FROM SCRATCH*

Pastor and Church Planter Matthew Brough once again provides thoughtful and engaging work to help us discover anew God's call upon both our lives and this beloved, yet broken world. Brough offers us hope that in our "sentness" we are not left on our own, but rather we participate and are transformed by what Jesus is doing in our midst - reconciling, redeeming and restoring life in all its abundance. You will put this book down ready and eager for your next assignment from God.

— ROSS LOCKHART, DEAN OF ST. ANDREW'S HALL, VANCOUVER, AND AUTHOR OF *BEYOND SNAKES AND SHAMROCKS: ST. PATRICK'S MISSIONAL LEADERSHIP LESSONS FOR TODAY.*

In this powerful book, Matt Brough reminds us with the Holy Spirit we have been given the power to go! We do not always know where we are going, if the timing is right, or if we are even properly equipped. None of this matters. The power of God will be at work through us. Our job is to trust the power and the authority of the Holy Spirit within. And Go! Highly recommended!

> — RICH LEWIS, AUTHOR OF *SITTING WITH GOD: A JOURNEY TO YOUR TRUE SELF THROUGH CENTERING PRAYER*

Drawn from a deep reservoir of pastoral leadership experience at the congregational, regional, and national levels, *Let God Send* presents a missional spirituality for ordinary people that is both winsome and compelling. Brough insists that those called to follow Jesus do not need to have all the answers, but they do need to be willing to risk taking the next step. This book will challenge congregations, small groups, and book clubs to do just that.

> — ROBERT J. DEAN, ASSOCIATE PROFESSOR OF THEOLOGY AND ETHICS, PROVIDENCE THEOLOGICAL SEMINARY AUTHOR OF *FOR THE LIFE OF THE WORLD* AND *LEAPS OF FAITH*

LET GOD SEND

CROSSING BOUNDARIES AND SERVING IN CHRIST'S NAME

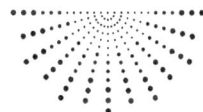

MATT BROUGH

Foreword by
J. DANA TRENT

Thicket Books

LET GOD SEND

Copyright © 2020 by Matthew David Brough. All rights reserved. Reproduction in whole or part of this publication without express written consent is strictly prohibited.

Edited by Lauren Craft, www.sharpeyeedits.net.

Unless otherwise noted, [Scripture quotations are from] New Revised Standard Version Bible: Anglicized Edition, copyright © 1989, 1995 National Council of the Churches of Christ in the United States of America. Used by permission. All rights reserved.

Scripture quotations marked MSG are taken from *THE MESSAGE*, copyright © 1993, 1994, 1995, 1996, 2000, 2001, 2002 by Eugene H. Peterson. Used by permission of NavPress. All rights reserved. Represented by Tyndale House Publishers, Inc.

CONTENTS

Foreword — 9
Introduction — 13

Part I
GOING

1. GOD'S UNPREDICTABLE PLANS — 25
   Realizing That You Are Sent — 25
   Circuitous Route — 27
   Stopped by the Spirit — 29

2. A WANDERING ARAMEAN — 35
   Abraham's Story — 35
   Where Am I Going? — 36
   God's Timing — 38
   Human-ness — 44

Part II
SENT WITH NOTHING EXCEPT AUTHORITY

3. BUT WE ONLY HAVE... — 51
   Low Resources for Going — 51
   Having Nothing—A Strategy for Trusting God — 53
   Spiritual Highs and Lows — 55
   You Feed Them — 58
   If Only We Had Jesus — 61
   But some doubted — 63
   Can We and Should We? — 65

4. YOU HAVE AUTHORITY — 71
   Authority and Therefore — 71

You Have Authority	73
It's Scary to Go for God	76

Part III
BE A MAKER

5. MAKE WHAT?	83
Make Disciples	83
What About Social Ministry?	88
6. WALKING ON SOMEONE ELSE'S TURF	93
Power Revisited	93
All the Way to the Ends of the Earth	97
Of All Nations	101

Part IV
RECLAIMING WITNESSING

7. YOU ARE A WITNESS	109
Teaching Obedience (Cringe)	109
Witnesses	113
A Witness Who Listens	116
Your Own Story to Tell	118
Reflection on the Man Born Blind	120
8. LISTENING, SEEING, TELLING	129
Place of Hope	129
Come and See is About a Person, not a Religion	133
Go...and Then	136
Resources for Connecting With God	141
Thank You	143
Other "Let God" Books	145
Acknowledgments	147
About the Author	149

FOREWORD

As I write this, our globe sits with despair. We have been ravaged by a virus, a crashing economy, and an ever-widening chasm between the poor and rich. The most vulnerable among us fear for their health while workers fear for their safety. The coronavirus pandemic has left us anxious, grieving, lost, and fearful. What good could possibly emerge from such chaos?

A call.

This book is a call amid the turmoil. Sacred scripture contains no shortage of narratives in which humans are pulled from their ordinary lives with an inciting incident whose stakes are high. These Biblical figures are lulled from complacency and comfort zones, and yet they are reluctant to serve because they question their ability and influence. Their lessons are relevant for us today. They, and we, are always called *and* sent with authority. The power of the Holy Spirit equips their "going"—and ours. It's a sending out that looks less like mastery and more

FOREWORD

like humility. It's a sending out that is unequivocal service to others modeled in a rabbi-reformer who washed feet and touched the unclean.

But will we let God send us? Matt Brough hopes so.

My own call to ministry came in with a reluctant "send" message. At age 21, I stood in the pews of my own rural Baptist Church as we belted out the Daniel Schutte invitational hymn written the year I was born, "Here I Am, Lord." Before that Sunday, I'd sung this hymn a million times, but these notes were distinct, "Whom shall I send?" The organ vibrated my bones; I felt pulled down the center aisle, treading the golden carpet beneath me, slowly, cautiously, as if I didn't know where I was headed. Just barely an adult, I arrived at the communion table to my smiling senior pastor. I didn't know what I was going to say, until it came out. "I feel called to ministry," I whispered, shocked at my own words, like I was speaking a foreign language.

I hadn't known it, but First Baptist Church's shepherds had been waiting for me to be "sent" the moment I crossed the sanctuary threshold when I was eleven years old. As the Bible teaches us, the moment of revelation doesn't arrive on its own. It is often birthed out of a circuitous path—a Holy Spirit led journey in which our calling is mirrored to us by those whom God has placed in our lives. Brough insists that we pay attention: How do we hold up the looking glass at each juncture? "Whom shall I send? Here I am, Lord."

Biblical and spiritual guides surround us; we merely need to heed their examples and insistence that God will not send us alone. Brough offers us the same: He is a steady companion in a discernment journey, providing us with a map of spiritual guides who show us how to offer gifts of presence and time to share Christ's love with others.

The religious landscape of North America is shifting. Will we open ourselves to the new ways in which we are called to be Christian in the 21st century and beyond? How will we answer the call? How will we be sent? Brough offers us thoughtful precautions: historic fire and brimstone sermons is not the call. Language of blame, sin, and guilt is not the call. Rather, the call is love: Jesus's "primary way of looking at human beings."

In his pastoral wisdom, Brough reminds us that there will be many "gos" along the way, always with "listening ears and a listening heart."

Let God Send invites us to listen, discern, see, and tell. This book asks us to consider the ways in which God calls us through God's people: people who stretch and strengthen us, people who challenge and confront us to consider the places in which we can serve in the "reality of people's lives."

Most importantly, through scripture, going, sending, making, and witnessing, Brough invites us into the way of Jesus. That way is love and empathy. We are not merely sent to "witness" but also to be witnessed to, especially by those different from ourselves. We are sent to be present in other's lives and spirituality, their journeys and struggles. We are sent to "places of hope," places where people are.

Our call is to lean into all the ways in which we are sent, even as we discern and sort out our personal, cultural, and religious baggage, in order to make room to receive the power of the Holy Spirit in our going. We are invited to remember the sacred narratives of those who have been sent before us with the authority and power of the Triune God.

What can come out of chaos?

A call.

May we let God send us. May we go. May we take steps directed by God, shining Jesus's love and compassion.

J. Dana Trent

March 2020

INTRODUCTION

YOU ARE SENT

I AM WITH YOU

Now the eleven disciples went to Galilee, to the mountain to which Jesus had directed them. When they saw him, they worshipped him; but some doubted. And Jesus came and said to them, 'All authority in heaven and on earth has been given to me. Go therefore and make disciples of all nations, baptizing them in the name of the Father and of the Son and of the Holy Spirit, and teaching them to obey everything that I have commanded you. And remember, I am with you always, to the end of the age.'

— MATTHEW 28:16-20

INTRODUCTION

When I was about twelve or thirteen years old, I was quite a good tennis player. I had only played against family and friends, but my level of play was starting to pass pretty much anyone I played, including adults. My parents encouraged me to take tennis lessons.

I refused to go, claiming that I only wanted to "play for fun." My parents didn't force the issue, and I was very glad for it. But I hadn't been honest with them about why I hadn't wanted to go. The truth was I was scared.

I had very low self-confidence as a teenager. I did not want to go into a new environment and meet a stranger. I didn't want to tell my parents about my fears because I thought I would sound silly. I thought that my fear would come across as an excuse that my parents would not accept. I thought that if I told them the truth, they would make me go and get lessons.

Deeper down, I was actually afraid to go to a lesson alone. For some reason, I imagined my parents dropping me off at a tennis club that I had never been to. I would have to fend for myself and figure out where to go and what to say. It never crossed my mind that my parents could go with me right onto the court. Because I didn't share my fears with them, it didn't cross their minds to tell me they would be there with me as much as I needed them.

At the end of Matthew's gospel, we discover that it did cross Jesus' mind to assure his disciples that he would always be with them.

I am still apprehensive in unfamiliar situations. There are times, as a pastor, when I get called to meet with a

INTRODUCTION

grieving family that I have not met before. Even after years of training and practice, I am still afraid to walk through the doors of an unfamiliar house into this kind of meeting. Every time I am in this situation, I pray for help. I have yet to be let down by Jesus.

Despite Jesus being there, it is not uncommon for Jesus-followers to feel ill-equipped or simply scared when prompted to take a step in ministry. We want the jobs he gives us to be someone else's job. We are afraid, not knowing what to say or do, not knowing who we might meet or whom we might be called to serve.

We either forget that Jesus, by the Holy Spirit, continues to be present through it all, or we somehow miss how powerful God's presence is. I pray that as you read through this short book about being sent by God, you will be reminded that you are not sent alone—Jesus is with you.

GO

In Genesis 12:1, Abram hears from God. God says to him, "Go from your country and your kindred and your father's house to the land that I will show you." God also promises Abram to make his name great but really gives him no further instructions than "go."

Abram set off and ended up in the land of Canaan. I suppose God was leading him, although we have no indication of that from the text itself. It is only after arriving that God confirms for him that it is indeed the Promised Land.

INTRODUCTION

The opening of Abram's story illustrates something very important for us. God asks us to go but doesn't usually reveal the destination. It is often only after we have arrived that we know that it was exactly where we were supposed to be.

When I was called by God to be a pastor, I didn't hear a distinct voice calling me to a specific congregation to serve. I remember, however, sensing God telling me to go to seminary. I hesitated over this call. I took the opportunity to ask others about it. Most people confirmed that I would "be a good pastor."

I shared a specific apprehension with one pastor whom I met at a youth conference. I told him that I wasn't sure about going to seminary because I couldn't imagine committing to being pastor "for the rest of my life." Even as I write it, I realize how foolish I was. He simply said, "You can only know what God is calling you to do today."

I realized in that moment that, until I heard otherwise, I should plan to go to seminary. That was what God had told me to do. While at seminary, I began sensing God's call to congregational ministry, then to a specific congregation. I served there for about three years when God shifted things again and called me to become a church planter.

Looking back on my time in seminary, I had been interested in church planting. In fact, many of the lessons I learned while volunteering in youth ministry, prior to going to seminary, were very useful in planting a church. The Spirit plants seeds to be used much further along the journey.

INTRODUCTION

Like Abram, we must respond to God sending us. We must go. It may not be to another country or to seminary. It may be to volunteer at church or at your kids' school. It may be to work at a homeless shelter or food bank. It may even be to renew your commitment to serving your spouse or to care for an aging parent. It may be to accompany someone who is struggling with grief.

Whatever it is, you are being called to go. You are being sent and you must make a move.

SENT IS WHO WE ARE

All human beings are created in the image of God. Followers of Jesus take this for granted. It is a given tenet of our faith, and it speaks to our individual value. We are not only precious to God, but we in some way reflect the character of God.

Some say being created in God's image is about our capacity for love. After all, God is love. Others speak about our being built for relationship because, of course, God's very self is defined as a loving relationship of Father, Son, and Spirit. Still others speak about God's care for creation, including God's care for people. Surely our being made in God's image is about the stewardship that we exercise on behalf of God, caring for our world and each other.

I want to say yes to all of these ideas about being made in God's image. Consider, as well, that being made in God's image also has something to do with being sent.

Jesus, as the "image of the invisible God" (Colossians

INTRODUCTION

1:15), was sent by the Father into the world. Throughout the gospel of John, Jesus consistently speaks of himself as sent by God. At the end of that same gospel, Jesus promises that the Holy Spirit would be sent to his disciples. Jesus also regularly speaks about the sending of his followers. This all comes together in John 20:21-22:

> *Jesus said to them again, 'Peace be with you. As the Father has sent me, so I send you.' When he had said this, he breathed on them and said to them, 'Receive the Holy Spirit.'*

Being sent is at the heart of Jesus' identity and he sends us, too! The idea of being sent gets at a particular quality of God. God is in motion. God is always and has always been moving toward us. God seeks us; God is interested in the world. God intervenes. Even in the act of creation itself, God's Spirit hovered right over the waters. God got down into the dirt to form Adam. God appeared in a burning bush when Moses wasn't looking for God at all. God whispered to Elijah on the mountain and thundered to Isaiah in the temple.

God is both the sender and the sent one. Jesus and the Spirit are sent by the Father. At least one of the persons of the Trinity is always on the go, always up to something.

When we look at how Jesus was sent, and then how he sent his first followers, we find that there is a clear purpose. Jesus pointed people to himself as the source of life, as the way, as the vine to which we all need connection. His disciples, once they were sent out, pointed not to themselves, but to Jesus. They healed people in his name; they proclaimed the good news in his name.

What does this look like for us if we also are sent by God? We are ambassadors—though Jesus is with us, and though the Holy Spirit goes before us, we are Jesus' representatives for others. Sometimes this means talking to someone about Christ. Sometimes this means serving and caring for someone as in Jesus' famous story of the Good Samaritan. Regardless of how it looks, we cannot avoid being sent people.

We might be more than a bit frightened to embrace our identity as sent-ones. We can be hesitant to go, to tell others about Jesus, to pray with or for another person, or to get out there and serve the needy in our world.

The truth is, God is sending you in a very specific way to very specific people, likely with a specific way of sharing the gospel in words and actions.

The Great Commission in Matthew 28:16-20 will be our guiding text. It is the quintessential sending story— Jesus sends out his closest followers to the ends of the earth with a specific mission.

This book is intended to provoke your thinking about your place in God's mission. I pray it will help you see things a little bit differently, in the hope that you may let go and allow God to do the sending. As you read it, perhaps you may begin sensing something specific from God. May you receive the courage of the Spirit to cross boundaries, overcome fear, and… **GO!**

QUESTIONS FOR REFLECTION OR DISCUSSION

1) Brough writes: "God asks us to go but doesn't usually reveal the destination. It is often only after we have arrived that we know that it was exactly where we were supposed to be." Has this been true for you? Has God ever asked you to take a step when the destination was unclear?

2) When you look back over your life what seeds do you see planted that God used later on in your own journey? This might be related to career path, relationships, volunteer opportunities, travel, education, or something else.

3) Jesus said "as the Father sent me, so I send you." How do you think this applies to your own sense of being sent?

4) Read 2 Corinthians 5:16-20. What do you think it means to be ambassadors for Christ?

5) When it comes to "going," we can be held back by fear. What kinds of things might someone be afraid of in responding to the sending call of God?

6) Think of a time you were outside of your comfort zone. This could be a time when you were serving in ministry some way, but it need not be. If you were alone, what difference would it have made to have someone alongside you? Reflect on what it means for Jesus to be with you.

PART I
GOING

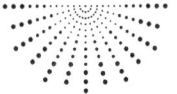

1

GOD'S UNPREDICTABLE PLANS

REALIZING THAT YOU ARE SENT

I KNOW some Christians who allow their lives to be directed by Jesus on a daily basis. I can't say that this is my personal experience. I simply don't consult Jesus about my every day or every minute actions.

When my sister calls and asks if I want to go to a Winnipeg Jets game (she has season tickets to our local National Hockey League franchise), I don't consult the Lord, nor do I think very hard. I just say "yes!" Then I check my calendar and see what I might need to re-arrange to be in the twelfth row shouting "Go Jets Go."

My point is, not every decision is God-guided, Spirit-inspired, or Jesus-led. I don't think every decision needs to be. I do, however, believe that God is the initiator. It is God who calls, God who sends, God who takes action on us, in us, and through us.

Realizing that God is sending you is one thing.

Knowing where to go, what to do, and then actually getting a move on can be much more complicated.

A few years ago, I was surprised when speaking with a small group in my congregation. We were discussing a kind of icebreaker question as group members were getting to know one another on the first night of a new program. The question was, "if you could ask God one question, what would it be?" Many people had questions about suffering—variations on "why does God allow bad things to happen to good people?" That question wasn't the surprise for me. What was surprising is that more than a few people had questions about their own personal purpose. They wanted to ask God, "what do you want me to do?" They seemed to have a sincere desire to "go for God" but recognized that it can be very hard to figure out what that looks like in real life.

It seems as though the first followers of Jesus had it easy, at least when it came to discerning what Jesus wanted them to do. Jesus came to them along the shores of the sea and asked them to follow him and fish for people. They went. After his resurrection, he sent them out, and they went. We don't always receive such clear direction.

Yet if you really think about it, even the first followers of Jesus had to discern and take risks as they took their first steps. When they left everything to follow Jesus, they didn't know what kind of life lay ahead of them. They likely didn't have much of a clue what "fishing for people" really meant. They were just drawn to Jesus. I have found this to be true in my own life as well.

For many years, I wanted to know God's plan for me, and, as a pastor, God's plan for our church. I would pray about it and make plans for the future based on where I thought God was leading. And then when those plans went sideways, I would pray and make more plans, and then more plans, and even more plans.

I still want to know where God is leading, and I still make plans, but I've also become less concerned about destinations, and much more concerned with the One with whom I'm travelling.

In the Great Commission, Jesus promised that his presence would go with the disciples. In Acts, we see this take shape through the coming of the Holy Spirit.

Knowing your exact calling, what God is asking you to do, is never as important as simply being with God. This is critical to grasp, because the life of "going," of being on a journey with Jesus and for God, of uncovering and living out your calling, is never simple or direct. Lord knows we need the Spirit's accompaniment on the journey.

CIRCUITOUS ROUTE

It turns out that the Bible is full of stories about journey, all of which take a long time and meander all over the place.

The disciples followed an itinerant rabbi named Jesus who, with no discernible pattern, wandered all over Galilee, Judea, and Samaria. The journeying seemed to be over when their master was killed. But then came the resurrection, the Great Commission, and the sending of his followers to the ends of the earth. Their journeying had only just begun. When the Holy Spirit showed up with power and purpose, the journey became even more wild and unpredictable.

Read, for example, the story of the calling of Saul in Acts 9. He was on his way to Damascus to arrest followers of Jesus and bring them back to Jerusalem as criminals. On the way, he was blinded and confronted by the resurrected Jesus and was led into the city where he spent three days and nights not eating or drinking.

God speaks to a disciple named Ananias, telling him to go to a particular house and find a man named Saul. At the same time, without Ananias' knowledge, God gives a vision to Saul of a man named Ananias healing him and restoring his sight.

Ananias questions where God is sending him: "Lord, I have heard from many about this man, how much evil he has done to your saints…" (Acts 9:13)

But God replies: "Go, for he is an instrument whom I have chosen to bring my name before Gentiles and kings…" (Acts 9:15)

Ananias remains skeptical. Nevertheless, he gets moving. He goes to the house, prays for Saul, who is healed and, from that day on, becomes known as Paul. He becomes the one sent by God throughout much of the known world, sharing the gospel, establishing churches, and eventually is the one who writes the majority of the New Testament.

God's plan for moving the message of Jesus beyond the

first few followers is circuitous and unpredictable. Often, we want a clear and direct plan for what God might have us do, but this is rarely how the Bible recounts God's plans.

While God was busy blinding Paul and challenging Ananias, I wonder if the other apostles were coming up with a strategic plan for how they would carry out the Great Commission and go to all the nations. If they were, wouldn't they have been surprised when their fiercest persecutor was suddenly the linchpin of the entire missionary operation to the gentiles!

Over and over, we discover that God's plans for sending us are radically different than our plans.

STOPPED BY THE SPIRIT

As we follow Paul's story, we discover it is full of stops and starts. Paul is always clear on the purpose of his mission, but there isn't always clarity about where to go.

In Acts 16:6-10, we find a very strange description about Paul and his fellow missionaries as they seek to go throughout the world to share the good news. The mission at this stage is to take the message about Jesus, particularly about his resurrection, to everyone. Surely, they should simply go everywhere, from town to town. But we discover that there are some regions that are off-limits. We are given no rationale for this, no explanation, other than the following verses:

> "They went through the region of Phrygia and Galatia, having been forbidden by the Holy Spirit to speak the word in Asia. When they had come opposite Mysia, they attempted to go into Bithynia, but the Spirit of Jesus did not allow them…"
>
> — ACTS 16:6-7

We often think that we need to spend a lot of time figuring out where God is sending us before we ever do anything. We think that discernment looks like a lot of prayer, planning meetings, reading books, getting educated, and doing all the necessary preparations. But we see very little preparation in the Bible. I'm all for good theological education, I'm all for prayer, I'm all for a good planning meeting, but not at the expense of making a move.

In Acts 16, we read about Paul and his companions on the move. It is *as they are going* that they receive direction from God. Note that the text says, "they attempted to go into Bithynia, but the Spirit of Jesus did not allow them." They tried, and for whatever reason God stopped them. It is okay to try. It is okay to risk.

As it turned out, what finally directed their movement was Paul having a dream of a Macedonian man asking for help. They set sail and ended up in the prominent Macedonian city of Philippi, where they met, not a man, but a woman named Lydia who helped establish the first church on European soil. This is the very gathering of people that Paul calls his "joy and crown," saints whom he loves and longs for (Phil. 4:1).

God's plans for the church in Philippi did not come to Paul fully formed, but that didn't stop him. He and his companions kept moving, and as they went, the steps along the way were revealed to them.

Rarely do we see the whole journey, with all of its twists and turns, mapped out before us. Instead, we are sent into the unknown, asked to take one step, then another, then another, often never quite knowing whether the move we are making is the "right one." But lack of clarity around what might be next must not hold us back from actually moving. We must go because God indeed is sending us.

QUESTIONS FOR REFLECTION OR DISCUSSION

1) Brough writes: "Knowing your exact calling, what God is asking you to do, is never as important as simply being with God." Describe a time in your life when this sentence describes your experience. Or describe a time when you wished you had rested in God's presence rather than worrying about an activity that you felt you were supposed to be doing.

2) Have you ever had a plan for your life that God has taken in an unexpected direction?

3) Can preparation and planning sometimes be a delay tactic for actually taking action? Are there any areas of your life where you are waiting for everything to be "just right" before you "make a move?"

4) Is unpredictability always a bad thing?

5) How can you approach God's plans for you as an adventure?

6) Is there anything in your life that seems meandering and aimless? How do you think God wants you to look at it?

7) In this chapter we read about God's plans to use Paul as an "instrument." Think of your favorite musical instrument and the music it plays. How much does it know about what the musician is planning to play? How can we apply this to God's work?

2

A WANDERING ARAMEAN

ABRAHAM'S STORY

THE STORY of the early Church is just one example of God sending His people. God's movement of sending is throughout the Bible, from Genesis to Revelation. God places Adam and Eve in the garden and gives them a mission to tend it. God sends Moses to Pharaoh to plead for the release of the Hebrew slaves. God sends his people from slavery to the Promised Land. God sends David to fight Goliath. We are in some ways used to the language of calling, but we can forget that a calling always requires the one being called to take action—to go. God always sends the one called to a particular people for a particular task. Think of the call of Samuel, who is sent as a prophet to the people. Think of the call of Isaiah, who is sent to proclaim God's message.

Over a number of years, I have been drawn to the story of Abraham, and I believe it is one of the most helpful biblical stories when thinking about a sending God in our current culture.

Three features of Abraham's story make it helpful for today:

1. He doesn't know where he is going.
2. He doesn't know when God's promise will be fulfilled, and it all takes a really long time.
3. He and his family are very human.

WHERE AM I GOING?

> Now the Lord said to Abram, "Go from your country and your kindred and your father's house to the land that I will show you..."
>
> — GENESIS 12:1

This is perhaps the ultimate example of God sending someone. God shows up in Abraham's life (this all took place before God had changed his name from Abram to Abraham), and with no context or conversation, God tells him to go! Three verses later, we discover that Abraham does it, seemingly with no questions asked: "So Abram went, as the Lord told him."

What is amazing to me is that Abraham has no clue where he is going. God gives him no direction other than what is found in verse 1. God will show Abraham the land that he is going to give to him and his descendants. That's it.

When you stop and think about what is going on here, it is pretty massive. This is the first mention in the Bible of the Promised Land. This land will dominate so much of the Bible's attention. This land will be the source of hope for the Hebrew slaves. This land will be fought over and protected. The future Israelites will be exiles from this land and will long for a return to it. They will return and rebuild, but it will be lost to world superpowers: Greece and then Rome. Throughout its history, this land will continue to be sought after as a place of holiness. As we know today, the Promised Land is still a place which people of varying religions and cultures claim as their own. All because God said to Abraham, "Go!"

You may claim that you don't usually hear God speaking. It's fine for Abraham to hear God, but that is not an everyday occurrence for most of us. Here's the thing—there is nothing in the Scriptures that indicates that this was an everyday occurrence for Abraham either. This is actually why I love this story so much!

The way the story reads, it sounds as if this all happened in one afternoon. God said, "Go to a land that I will show you," and Abraham essentially said, "Okay" and started packing his things. Maybe that is exactly what happened. Or maybe what is recorded as a quick conversation was actually several years of sensing something, or months of Abraham trying to ignore a feeling nagging away at him. Maybe Abraham and his wife, Sarah, had conversation after conversation about moving. Maybe they were already resolved to leave Haran but just needed assurance that God would guide them in the journey.

If we take the Bible at face value, the first time Abraham heard from God is the year that he turned seventy-five. When we say, "God doesn't speak to me," consider the actual story that is told in Scripture. Abraham's adventures in being sent started at seventy-five. Who knows what God has in store for you? Well, God does!

I just love the way God works! So unexpected.

GOD'S TIMING

The fact that Abraham is seventy-five years old when his story starts tells us a couple of things: 1) God's timing is not our timing, and 2) God may be a bit of a comedian (as every comedian knows, timing is everything, and God has perfect timing).

By the time we get ten verses into his story in Genesis 12, Abraham and his family have already arrived in Canaan. God reveals that this is in fact the land that he is giving to Abraham. Abraham builds an altar to God and calls on God's name—he worships and gives thanks. Despite the land being occupied by the Canaanites, our hero has arrived at his destination. God sent. Abraham went. Land has been found. Done deal.

But then verse ten happens. In verse ten, we discover that there is a problem. "Now there was a famine in the land. So Abram went down to Egypt to reside there as an alien, for the famine was severe."

But wait a second. If God knew about a drought that would make the Promised Land unliveable (a place that later will be called a land flowing with milk and honey!), why did God send Abraham when he did? Why not just let Abraham and his family live in Haran and ride out the drought? Maybe they would have had to go to Egypt for food anyway, but isn't it a bit cruel to show them the land (occupied land at that!) and then have weather conditions that make it impossible to settle there?

What is God up to? The short answer is that God has different timing than we do. Abraham really struggles with this, however, as we shall see.

Eventually, after all kinds of ups and downs, Abraham and Sarah make it back to the Promised Land of Canaan. In Genesis 15, God renews the covenant made in Genesis 12, being much more explicit about the land and the promise of Abraham's descendants. This time, Abraham talks back to God. In fact, God being more explicit about the covenant with Abraham is a response to Abraham questioning him.

> After these things the word of the Lord came to Abram in a vision, "Do not be afraid, Abram, I am your shield; your reward shall be very great." But Abram said, "O Lord God, what will you give me, for I continue childless, and the heir of my house is Eliezer of Damascus?" And Abram said, "You have given me no offspring, and so a slave born in my house is to be my heir."

— GENESIS 15:1-3

Right after this, God promises Abraham that he will indeed have a son and his descendants will be as many as the stars. This promise from God is one that is so central to the Judeo-Christian tradition. It is a promise that is returned to time and time again. We are then explicitly told that Abraham believed God and, "the Lord reckoned it to him as righteousness" (Genesis 15:6). This short verse has been used to show the importance of faith, and in particular, how Abraham was a true model of having faith. God recognizes Abraham's faith and reckons it (i.e. counts it) as righteousness. In other words, it isn't Abraham's actions that make him right with God, but it is his faith in God and God's promise that are counted as though he had actually been righteous in all his living.

Perhaps because Christians so often stress the importance of Abraham's faith, and God's declaration of his faith making him right, we often don't think about or miss the rest of what God tells Abraham in this passage. We either forget about it, or we don't think about it in the context of Abraham's life and calling. God tells him that he will have numerous descendants but that they will eventually be aliens in a foreign land and will be oppressed there for four hundred years. After that God will bring them out, and then they will come back to the Promised Land in the fourth generation.

Imagine getting that kind of news from God after being asked to completely uproot your family and move.

LET GOD SEND

You've gone through all kinds of trials in foreign lands, you finally make it back to the land of promise, and God promises children and long life for you, but also says that the overall purpose won't be seen until long after your death! Granted Abraham's life is not all bad. He does become pretty wealthy, and lives a nice long life, despite all his misadventures. Still, the core promise to Abraham will take what seems like an unreasonably long time to come to pass.

After the promise about having lots of descendants and God apparently not delivering on this promise in the timeframe they want, Abraham and Sarah take matters into their own hands in trying to produce an heir. Because they have been unsuccessful in conceiving, they plan for Abraham to sleep with Sarah's slave, Hagar. Yes, this is exactly what it sounds like. Not good.

Ishmael is born to Hagar, and we are told in Genesis 16:16 that Abraham is now eighty-six years old. These age markers are important because we can see that Abraham, like all of us, is impatient and feels like time is running out. Of course it is! Even with a promise from God to live to a good old age, Abraham is eighty-six before he has his first son.

Flip to chapter 17, and we find that Abraham has aged thirteen more years. We have no indication of what happened in those thirteen years. Almost certainly, Abraham has felt that the question of an heir and the promise of descendants has been taken care of. His son, Ishmael, is just about to become a man as he is turning thirteen. God had provided a son (with a bit of scheming from Abraham and Sarah) so that the promise could be fulfilled.

But then God shows up again, and the covenant is renewed once more. At the age of ninety-nine, Abraham receives instructions about a sign that will bind the covenant to Abraham and his descendants. The men are all to be circumcised. And then, in Genesis 17:15-22, God spells out that Sarah will have a son, and that the covenant will be established through her child. God tells Abraham that he should be named Isaac, which means "he laughs."

Abraham, of course, argues with God, being much more forceful than their previous conversations. Abraham pleads for his son, Ishmael, and questions whether Sarah at ninety years old can bear children. God laughs, naming the child after his comedy or perhaps after their shared joy to come through the child. What becomes clear in the story is that it is God making the decisions, with perfect timing, and it is all so different than the way Abraham would have planned it.

In Genesis 18, the laughing continues. This time, it is Sarah who is listening to her husband talk to the three visitors (sometimes they seem like angels, sometimes they are referred to as "The Lord" - or possibly just one of them is "The Lord"). One of the visitors announces that when he returns the following season, Sarah will have a son. Sarah hears it and laughs to herself. The words from Genesis tell it best:

 The Lord said to Abraham, "Why did Sarah laugh, and say, 'Shall I indeed bear a child, now that I am old?' Is anything too wonderful for the Lord? At the set time I will return to you, in due season, and Sarah shall have a son." But Sarah denied, saying, "I did not laugh"; for she was afraid. He said, "Oh yes, you did laugh."

— GENESIS 18:13-15

This is so great! Have you ever seen a comedian do a bit where they are playing it deadpan, and the audience is killing themselves laughing? Then, they stop the bit and turn to the audience and ask, "Why are you laughing? I'm not joking!" The audience breaks up all the more. This is how I imagine God in this story.

Sarah laughs at the ridiculousness of the situation, and God knows as well as she does that it is indeed funny. But he calls her out because God isn't making things up as he goes. God is declaring truth and, on the surface, it is laughable—but it is also joyful. It's as if God is saying, "Why are you laughing? Don't you believe I can do anything?" The difference from the comedian doing a bit is that this is God, and there is some fear and trembling. Sarah doesn't respond with more laughter, but instead, denies it. She's afraid. "I didn't laugh," she says. "Oh, yes, you did!" God basically says, "Gotcha!"

Notice in this whole story that the people are trying to take action in their stumbling kind of ways, but in the end, it is God who moves everything along. And God's timing is not our timing. God's got perfect timing.

HUMAN-NESS

Despite God being overwhelmingly present in Abraham and Sarah's story, their lives are very human lives. Actually, I say God is overwhelmingly present, but in Scripture, we only get the highlights. Years, sometimes decades, pass before we read of an encounter between Abraham and God. This, too, is the human experience.

When I first became a pastor in the Presbyterian Church, I was surprised to learn about people's experiences of God. Presbyterians don't tend to talk very much about their spiritual experiences. We will barely talk about how we pray or read the Bible. In the pastor role, I ended up being in a position to hear people's stories and, in those first few years of ministry, a number of people did, in fact, share stories about God showing up and being present in their lives. At the time, I didn't pay too much attention. Many of the stories were from older people looking back on earlier times in their lives. I wrote these stories off as a very long time ago. I should have paid closer attention and given their stories and the people much greater honor.

The reality is that many of us experience God in some way at one or more points in our lives. Experiencing God is a human reality, and it is reflected in Abraham and Sarah's story.

Alongside their monumental faith and the trust that Abraham and Sarah learn to place in God, a number of other elements are part of their story. They are at times uncertain. They take matters into their own hands. They make some big mistakes. They experience the pain of not being able to have children. They experience the confusion of uprooting and living in a foreign culture. Abraham and Sarah, like all people depicted in Scripture, are flawed, broken, human.

Why do I point out their human-ness? Because we need reminding that God sends very human people. It is helpful to have the right perspective on the spiritual giants of Scripture. They were people, and when you go and read their stories, their humanity is abundantly evident.

God is not looking for super-humans, and God is not sending only the ultra-spiritual that always feel a connection to him. Why not? Because those people don't exist, and the ones seen as "spiritual giants" are often the first to tell us so.

God sends people with broken families. God sends people who experience confusion and doubt. God sends people who are very old (and very young). God sends people who think they know better than he does at times. God sends people who are impulsive. God sends people who make poor choices.

It's not that we should purposely try to be broken, as though that makes us extra human. It's that we cannot allow our human-ness to disqualify us. In fact, none of the three features pointed out in Abraham's story ought to stop us from making a move in response to God sending us.

1. We don't always know where we are going—neither did Abraham.
2. The timing isn't right—tell that to Abraham and Sarah!
3. We feel like we have too many problems or our lives are messy—just look at the servants God sent in Scripture. Abraham and Sarah were just regular, very human people.

QUESTIONS FOR REFLECTION OR DISCUSSION

1) It has become cliché to say "God's timing is not our timing." Does this ring true for you? Are there times when this doesn't apply or when it is not helpful?

2) Are Abraham and Sarah impatient? Why or why not?

3) Sometimes God's plans seem ridiculous (Sarah laughs at the idea of her having a child), but the fulfilment of God's plans are also joyful and perhaps playful (also represented by laughter). Do you know any other examples of God's plans seeming both ridiculous and joyful from the Bible? From history? From your own life?

4) Can you think of a time when you have experienced the presence of God in a tangible or powerful way? Did God communicate anything, or did you learn anything through the encounter?

5) Do you ever feel unworthy to be used by God? Why? How do you think God sees you?

6) Do you suppose your "human-ness" or brokenness could be an asset in God's work? If so, how?

PART II
SENT WITH NOTHING EXCEPT AUTHORITY

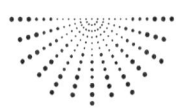

3

BUT WE ONLY HAVE...

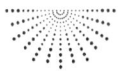

LOW RESOURCES FOR GOING

 Now the eleven disciples went to Galilee...

— MATTHEW 28:16

When the disciples come together to receive the Great Commission, there are only eleven of them. Jesus is about to tell them to go to the entire world. Their task is massive, and they are very few in number. Anytime we are discouraged by our lack of resources, whether it is less money, dwindling volunteers, or even discouraged hearts, we need look no further than this text—though many biblical stories also emphasize God doing great things with very little.

One of my favorites is the story of Gideon. God called Gideon at a time when the people of Israel were under military occupation by a foreign power. When God first spoke to Gideon through an angel, he called him a "mighty warrior." Gideon's response was to explain to the angel that he was not mighty at all: "My clan is the weakest... and I am the least in my family" (Judges 6:15).

Even once God convinces Gideon to go and fight against their oppressors, it remains a story about God doing wonders through smallness. Judges 7 tells the story of how 32,000 Israelites rallied to Gideon to fight, but then God continued to say, "The troops with you are too many" (Judges 7:2). More and more troops are sent home until only 300 remain. God tells Gideon the reason he doesn't want a large fighting force is that the Israelites would be able to take credit for their victory. If there are only 300 troops and they still win, they will surely give all of the credit to God alone.

When we are sent by God in mission with little to nothing, it builds our trust, but it also strengthens our witness to the power of God at work through us.

We can be tempted to not take a step until everything is perfectly aligned. We think we need curriculum, training, vast volunteer armies, charismatic leaders, and plenty of money in the budget. But the time when we are "weak" may be the best time to respond to God sending us out. This way, success is only possible through radical trust in God, and the power of God will be all the more evident.

This line of thinking is often found in the stories of the people that God consistently calls throughout Scripture. Mary, a young girl of no real consequence, is chosen as the mother of Jesus, who is born, not in splendor and majesty, but in a small town, and laid among the straw of a feed trough. The first witnesses and heralds of the miraculous birth of the King of Kings are not governors or princes, but lowly shepherds who just happened to be living nearby.

Over and over again, God chooses regular people: shepherds, fishermen, tax collectors, though none of them are particularly well-equipped for their tasks.

Even at the end of years of training with Jesus, his group of disciples is still small and fragile. Just eleven gathered for their "great" commissioning.

If for a moment we believed that the Great Commission was some idyllic scene, we must not forget why there are only eleven and not twelve disciples. Judas was among them until his terrible betrayal and then his suicide.

The eleven is not just a small number; it is a number that brings up their incompleteness and their very real pain. A friend had turned on their Lord and then turned away from life itself. These eleven disciples had to live with the pain of that, and yet, they are still commissioned, and we know that they went.

The conditions of our lives will never be perfect to respond to the sending call of God.

HAVING NOTHING—A STRATEGY FOR TRUSTING GOD

> He said to them, 'Take nothing for your journey, no staff, nor bag, nor bread, nor

> money—not even an extra tunic. Whatever house you enter, stay there, and leave from there. Wherever they do not welcome you, as you are leaving that town, shake the dust off your feet as a testimony against them.' They departed and went through the villages, bringing the good news and curing diseases everywhere.
>
> — LUKE 9:3-6

These are Jesus' seemingly ludicrous instructions to his twelve closest followers as he sent them out to proclaim the kingdom and heal people. His primary strategy for success is for them to take nothing with them.

What is it that powers the disciples' participation in God's mission? What gives them the ability to actually do what Jesus asks them to do? Only God.

They have to trust that God will provide for them. They have to trust that Jesus was telling the truth when he said that he was giving them all power and authority.

Who lives like that? I don't know about you, but I have trouble trusting Jesus that much.

But here is what I love… When you feel ill-equipped to talk to a neighbor about Jesus, when you aren't sure if you should invite someone needing encouragement to your home for a meal, when you don't know if you should serve at your city's food bank or homeless shelter, when you don't think you can really do what the voice of the Holy Spirit in your mind is asking you to do, remember this—you are not supposed to have any resources at your disposal: no money, no food, no change of clothes. You are supposed to be utterly dependent on God to provide what's necessary for you as you go where the Spirit is sending you.

But there is *something* that you do have. You have the power and the authority of Jesus Christ to do his ministry in your life and in the world. He has called you to him, and he is sending you out with his authority and power to do his will in serving others.

The twelve went with no resources, no study guides, no processes to follow, no job descriptions. Sometimes, it didn't work. There were towns where they were not welcomed. When that happened, they weren't deterred. They simply shook the dust off their feet and left the village as they found it. They moved on to the next place and tried again. The end result was that the gospel was proclaimed and people were healed almost everywhere they went.

SPIRITUAL HIGHS AND LOWS

Imagine how awesome, thrilling, and perhaps a little terrifying it would have been to be one of the twelve. Imagine having gone into village after village with nothing. Imagine having experienced the power and authority of Jesus working through you for people to hear the good news and receive healing. Imagine the stories you would have to share. Imagine how your perspective on faith and life would change after trusting

God to provide like that, and then seeing the kind of results they saw.

We are told in Luke 9:10 that when the apostles (which means "sent-ones," by the way) returned, they intended to give Jesus a report. They withdrew to a solitary place to be alone together, but the crowd followed them.

Jesus then does more of what he had already been doing in his ministry. He welcomes the crowd, speaks to them about the kingdom of God, and heals anyone who needs healing.

The twelve had these life-changing experiences of going out, trusting in God's provision, speaking to people about Jesus and the kingdom, and healing people. They had received Jesus' authority and power, and it had worked. But then, this…

> The day was drawing to a close, and the twelve came to him and said, 'Send the crowd away, so that they may go into the surrounding villages and countryside, to lodge and get provisions; for we are here in a deserted place.'
>
> — LUKE 9:12

Maybe they were tired. Just back from a successful mission trip, they have returned to be with Jesus: to be renewed by him. Likely they were looking for some alone time with him, perhaps a nice hot meal and some wise words from their teacher. Being with Jesus was, of course, the call that they had originally answered. They had just been used by God in remarkable ways, and that was great and all, but seeing Jesus do what *he* does, now that's awesome. Perhaps they just wanted to be close to Jesus, because that is the ultimate experience.

That's what we often want as his followers, isn't it? We want to simply go to our worship services in peace. We would love quiet time with Jesus if we could get it. Some of us may go to Bible studies or prayer meetings, or conferences, or retreats. We need to "recharge" from all our busy-ness in life. We need our spirits to have renewal so we can face the world.

This line of thinking leads very easily to a separation of our "spiritual" life from our "real" life. We have our time with Jesus, and we have our time in the world. We start *using* Jesus to get us through our life. We begin thinking that the Church exists for us to have some spiritual fuel to get through the week. We may say things like, "I like coming to church to get a good sermon, or to sing the songs, or to have some time to pray." We start believing that the Church is there for "me."

But Jesus was doing something different. He was creating a Church full of people who were there for others. The gathering was not a time for the individuals to get spiritual energy just to get through their week. The gathered Church was the location of being equipped to go out and participate in God's mission in the world. The Church's purpose is not to help you get *through* your life. Rather, as part of the Church, you are part of a people who are gathered to be equipped and then sent out to serve.

YOU FEED THEM

The disciples just had an awesome mission trip. They're tired. They want time with Jesus. They tell Jesus to send the crowds away because they are in a remote place, and the people are going to need to eat.

> But he said to them, 'You give them something to eat.'
>
> — LUKE 9:13

This is Christian service. We have experiences of God using us, and we think, "That changed my life—that was awesome." And then a day later, God is asking us to do something else.

What are the disciples thinking here? I think it might go something like this: "God—you just changed my life with that first thing you asked me to do! *Really*, my heart is yours. I went into the villages and proclaimed your message! I healed people in your power! It was awesome. But *these* people can buy their own food. *They* don't really need me. *These* people can hear more teaching tomorrow —just send them to go get something to eat somewhere else. They're not really our responsibility. They're capable people. They're responsible for themselves."

And Jesus says, "You feed them."

So, were the disciples' hearts *really* changed on their mission trip? Did the sending out with a mission accomplish anything in them? The disciples behave as though they are done with their mission, not realizing that following Jesus means that the mission trip continues even after you return home.

I can't blame the disciples for their behavior. I would do the same. Any of us would. After an exhausting and intense time of serving people in God's name, I would want some quiet time. In other places in Scripture, we are taught that rest is very important. It is even embedded in one of the ten commandments.

We forget that rest is always a gift. Instead, we treat rest as something we earn through hard work. We say things like "I deserve a rest." Here, Jesus does not allow rest to be treated this way. The disciples were being trained on their mission trip, and there is more work to do. Rest will come, that is for certain. But it will come not as a reward for faithfulness or hard work, but as a gift.

After Jesus says, "you feed them," the disciples argue with Jesus. They tell him that they only have five loaves and two fish to feed five thousand. This is where Jesus takes control, using and further training his disciples to be ministers (literally, servants).

Jesus starts by getting the twelve to do crowd control. He tells them to make sure everyone is sitting on the grass in groups of fifty.

Jesus gives thanks for the food and then gets his disciples to distribute it. There is enough for everyone. After everyone has eaten their fill, Jesus sends his disciples among the crowd to collect the leftovers.

I'm always struck by the simple fact that Jesus is not the one who went out to distribute the food. He simply told his disciples what to do, and they followed his instructions. The feeding of the five thousand would not normally be thought of as a story about God sending us, but this is, in fact, exactly what Jesus does. He sends his disciples to the groups of fifty to feed them.

The text doesn't say when the food multiplied. I like to think it happened as the distribution took place. I like to think that Jesus gave his disciples just the five loaves and two fish, and they had to walk to the first group of fifty on faith that it would all work out. I like to think that the disciples had to trust Jesus, trust that somehow God would provide.

In the previous story, Jesus sends his disciples with no food, and no extra clothes. Here, Jesus sends them with just a few meager portions.

When we are sent by Jesus to serve others, we may feel as though our energy reserves are low, or that we do not have the necessary resources. We will almost always feel ill-equipped. This is exactly how we should feel as a follower of Jesus because it means that any good thing that takes place through our service must be attributed to God.

The disciples fed the crowd, but it was Jesus that did the miracle. If we only serve others when we have all the necessary resources, or when we feel comfortable, then we will begin believing in, and relying on, ourselves to transform people's lives and the world. This is, in the end, a misplaced trust. Our reliance must rest squarely on God.

We often miss what God is capable of. We forget about trusting God even after we have seen displays of his power. Even after the disciples had received power and authority from Jesus, even after spending countless hours with him, even after a successful mission trip, they can't see what they should do next to serve others. The disciples can't envision how to do ministry in their life. They can't see the power of Jesus to feed the entire crowd with only a few loaves and fish.

Our vision for going and serving must be transformed to one of possibility and one of trust in God.

IF ONLY WE HAD JESUS

Good Christians look at the feeding of the five thousand story and shake their heads. The disciples are so naive, so short-sighted, so unfaithful, we think. They had Jesus right there!

If we had Jesus with us, we wouldn't send people away, we claim. If we had Jesus with us, we would be feeding all the hungry there were. If we had Jesus with us, we'd be boldly asking him to heal the sick. If we had Jesus with us, we'd be shouting the good news from the rooftops. How can the disciples possibly suggest sending people away when they've got Jesus right there?

But why would we ever say, "*if* we had Jesus with us?" We do have Jesus with us!

Our issue is that we act as though Jesus *isn't* with us. Sometimes we act as though Jesus is with us in church, but not with us when we get a feeling that we should invite our friend to church. Sometimes we suppress our inner promptings that urge us to reach out to encourage someone, or to start something, or volunteer somewhere, or serve the poor in our city. We try to bury those thoughts and try to not feel guilty. In other words, we act as though Jesus isn't really here.

Actually, the disciples were much better than we usually are. They knew that if they were going to send the people away, they had to ask Jesus first. Only Jesus had the authority to dismiss the crowd.

We usually have numerous opportunities to serve others, but we rarely even consult Jesus about those opportunities. When faced with someone begging on the streets, do we at the very least pray, asking Jesus what he wants us to do? When a call for volunteers goes out from our kids' school, do we ask the Lord whether the call might be for us? When a moment to practically love and serve others is presented, I tend to ask whether I want to do it, have the time to do it, or whether it is "really the right thing to do for me," but rarely do I turn those thoughts into active prayer. I believe that we don't consult Jesus because we generally don't want to give Jesus that kind of control over our lives.

At least the disciples, with Jesus physically standing in their midst, couldn't get away with what we consider to be the normal behavior of avoiding opportunities to serve in his name.

BUT SOME DOUBTED

 When they saw him, they worshipped him but some doubted.

— MATTHEW 28:17

This is one of the most remarkable phrases in the Bible. At this point, the risen Jesus has already appeared to his disciples several times. It is only the eleven core disciples here. It is the inner circle, but some of them doubted? This kind of shocks me, though I suppose it shouldn't. We all have doubts.

I can't help wondering, though, what exactly they were doubting. I don't think that they were doubting that Jesus was really there. They could see and touch him. I don't think that there were two or three disciples who started thinking they were having a group hallucination.

I wonder if maybe some of them were doubting Jesus' true identity. The fact that this verse is about worship might lead us in that direction. They worshipped him and Jesus let them, which is extremely significant. Worship is reserved only for God, so unless Jesus is God, they should stop what they are doing.

I wonder, though, if related to any doubts about Jesus' identity, there might have been some doubts about what would be next. The resurrection had happened, but life seemed to be continuing on as usual for most people. Was Jesus going to just wander around Galilee, Judea, and

Samaria some more, telling people "I'm back! Death is defeated!"?

Whatever the exact doubts, and despite the shock of this albeit minority reaction, I am also encouraged by this verse. Some of the eleven doubted. That means, if I have doubts, that's normal. It is normal to have doubts even as you are worshiping the Living Christ.

Jesus doesn't just commission those with perfect or unwavering faith. In fact, none of his disciples, as described in the gospels, show themselves to be perfect believers or followers.

While on the mountain at the end of Matthew's gospel, Jesus does not say, "I am sending you seven disciples because you have got it the most right. You four need to work on your doubt problem first, then you can go." Jesus just sends all of them, doubters included.

If you have any doubts about Jesus, you can still be sent by him. Go anyway. You can still serve. You can still talk with someone about Jesus, or about your faith. Talk to people about your doubt if you like.

In today's climate and culture, it may even be an advantage to be a bit of a doubter. I'm by no means encouraging you to harbor doubts or to linger in doubt for very long. However, it can be a real turn off to non-Christians to talk with a Jesus follower who is overly self-assured. Someone who is willing to explore, ask questions, and be patient—someone who understands skepticism—is much more likely to relate well to today's non-believer.

The good news is, we all have doubts at one time or

another. Perhaps the real surprise of this text is that it says that only *some* doubted.

CAN WE AND SHOULD WE?

The disciples do, in fact, care that the people don't have enough to eat. They believe that something must happen. Their solution is to send them away. All the people would be able to go into town and get something to eat. The disciples have a few loaves and fish, so they could have a quiet, relaxing meal with Jesus.

What we should not miss is that the disciples actually see the need of the people, have compassion for them, and know something must be done. More often than not, we know there is need out there, but we still do little to nothing about it.

- We know there is vast poverty in our own city or town.
- We know people in our lives who are struggling with loneliness, anxiety, or family conflict.
- We know people who don't know the blessing of God or who have a warped picture of the love of Jesus.
- We know people who are sick and need healing and comfort.

But perhaps, like the disciples, we conclude that responding to their need is not something we are going to do, either because it is not really our responsibility, or because we don't have the resources. We see and care about people in need, but for a variety of reasons, we don't believe we can or should do anything about it.

Can we do anything? This is the question of power. Are we able—do we have the power to do anything?

Should we do anything? This is the question of authority. Are we the ones to go? What gives us the right, and is this our responsibility?

Jesus doesn't gather us to give us just enough spiritual fuel to get us through to the next time of worship. He gathers us to equip us, by the working of the Holy Spirit, to be sent out with his authority and power to do his will, to serve others in our lives.

It is hard though, isn't it? Because try as we might, we often don't quite believe that we have the power and authority of Christ.

We also have trouble really believing that Jesus' authority is over everything and that Jesus' power can transform the most desperate of situations. We can't quite grasp that he will use us to work on the needs he's placed on our hearts. Our vision of what God will do through us as his servants is limited by our fears, our rationality, our self-centeredness, our sense of inadequacy, our busy-ness, and countless other things.

These things that hold us back are difficult to deal with, and they are all the more reason to gather together each week to be reminded and encouraged in our service. These are all the more reason to go to Jesus with our weak faith and ask for something more. These are all the more reason to give ourselves over to him and his mission, all the more reason to really trust Jesus with our lives. All the more reason to let his Spirit go to work in us and through us for the benefit of this world for which Jesus died and rose again—this world that God loves so much.

QUESTIONS FOR REFLECTION OR DISCUSSION

1) Are there times when you feel you cannot "go" because you don't have enough resources or because the conditions aren't quite right?

2) Can you think of a time when something great happened through something small?

3) How do you respond to the idea that, though you may feel like you have little to nothing, you have the power and authority of Christ?

4) Are there times when you have expected church (or even Jesus) to exist to meet your needs? How might God be shifting you to see yourself as part of a church that exists to go out and serve?

5) In the story of the loaves and fish, the disciples ask Jesus what to do even though they have a preferred

solution in mind already. How can you follow their example?

6) What sorts of needs exist in your community?

7) Brough writes: "Our vision for going and serving must be transformed to one of possibility and one of trust in God." Do you ever find it difficult to have an outlook of possibility? Do you ever find it difficult to truly trust God? What steps might you take to trust more?

8) How would you understand the significance that some of the disciples doubted as they worshipped Jesus and that Jesus then sent the doubters? What does it mean for you if you have some doubts? What does it mean for you in how you treat others who have doubts?

4

YOU HAVE AUTHORITY

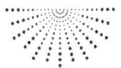

AUTHORITY AND THEREFORE

> And Jesus came and said to them, 'All authority in heaven and on earth has been given to me…'
>
> — MATTHEW 28:18

IN THIS PASSAGE, where Jesus gives his disciples the Great Commission, Jesus acts as Lord, as King. He can command his subjects to do as he says because of his universal claim of having authority over everything in heaven and on earth.

While we regularly speak about Jesus as Lord, the image of "lord" can be difficult to relate to. We don't interact with many kings or lords these days, and even what we do see of them, it is usually a figurehead role. In addition, we have so many examples of authority being mis-used by those in positions of power or trust, making it even harder for us to grasp onto this way of thinking. We can instantly name situations were ministers, parents, police officers, or government officials have abused, harmed, manipulated, or murdered people and have used their positions of authority to do it.

Because of this very real pain, it can be tempting to ignore images of authority and focus instead solely on other ways of talking about Jesus, such as friend, companion, sibling, or servant. In making this move, however, we miss the power in Jesus' upending of our usual notions of how authority is exercised. Jesus washed his disciples' feet, he served, he humbled himself, and this is incredibly powerful for the very reason that Jesus is Lord over all.

The reality that Jesus is Lord means that when we claim to follow him, we must also be honest with ourselves about how we are responding to what he tells us to do. Here, Jesus reminds us that he has all authority and then follows it up in verse nineteen with the first two words that are properly part of the actually commissioning of the Great Commission: "Go therefore." We would do well to pay attention to the one with all authority, especially when he gives us a direct command, like "go." The disciples are to go not just because of their loyalty to Jesus, or because of their friendship, but because Jesus has the authority to send them.

This may seem painfully obvious, but how much time do we really devote to thinking about this? Because here is the real question for anyone who might be a little hesitant about being sent: are you really behaving as though Jesus has all authority? If Jesus is sending you, and he has full authority over everything, what is holding you back from going as he asks?

YOU HAVE AUTHORITY

> Then Jesus called the twelve together and gave them power and authority over all demons and to cure diseases
>
> — LUKE 9:1

In the Great Commission, Jesus reminds his disciples that he has authority over everything, but the disciples have heard about and witnessed Jesus' authority before. Jesus' authority over evil spirits and his authority to heal people was on display from day one of his ministry. In Luke 9, something remarkable happens: the twelve disciples are granted authority to do what, up until that point, only Jesus had been doing. Jesus doesn't reserve his authority for himself—he shares it with his disciples.

It can be tempting to limit the conferral of authority to only this moment and only these twelve. We balk at the idea of Jesus giving us, today, similar authority. I believe he does, even though I do not see miraculous healing everywhere I go, nor are there everyday occasions to cast out evil spirits, at least, not for me.

If we are given authority in a similar way, then why do

we not see better results from the ministry in which we may be engaged? My own belief is that most of the time, we are not acting out of our Christ-given authority. Either we are too timid, or when we act boldly, we are doing it in such a way that it is not in service to others, but is far too self-serving.

We will see boldness in the name of Christ from corners of the Christian faith, but those same corners can often be aligning themselves with one political agenda or another. We sometimes see leaders claiming the authority of Christ in order to cast the first stone of condemnation, claiming a moral high-ground on one issue or another, rather than bringing a word of hope where comfort and healing is needed. We can misuse Christ's authority when our only motive for our boldness is something like increasing our numbers in church or increasing our offerings.

I am not saying that Christians should not make political statements or proclaim moral teaching, nor am I saying that we shouldn't employ strategies for church growth (though, I will remind you that Christian opinion on all of these matters varies widely).

We must look at the context of the authority that Christ gave his followers. They were given authority "over all demons and to cure diseases." Many of us are skeptical about evil spirits or faith-healings. Rather than try and convince you about anything related to these categories, I will merely point out that the activity of the disciples had to involve actual encounters with real people.

LET GOD SEND

Their area of authority was one that addressed human need. In their time, there was a real fear of evil spirits. Anyone who had an evil spirit was to be avoided. So too, anyone with a disease (like leprosy, for example) was to be avoided. Jesus, instead, gave them authority in two areas that would enable them to enter the world of those who were suffering the most—those believed to be possessed, and those who were terribly sick. Because of this new authority, the disciples would be able to speak to and serve even those who were deemed unclean and untouchable.

The examples of this kind of ministry today don't tend to make the headlines. Perhaps the most widely known example in recent history of someone acting with this kind of authority is Mother Teresa. She worked with, touched, and loved those whom many of us would usually avoid.

But we don't need to go as big as Mother Theresa. We only need to look in our own cities and towns. We simply need to visit the places where people are hurting the most and you will almost always find others there as well. Usually they are at outposts of hope, providing food or shelter to the homeless. Many of the people at these outposts are followers of Jesus, acting out of his shared authority. He tells them to go and they do go, every day, every week, being bold in serving those whom Christ loves so dearly. It is always remarkable to me how our western and northern culture has become more and more secular, yet the majority of non-government organizations that continue to work with the poor are in fact Christian-based or at least have strong Christian roots.

Yet, we don't need to go to the poorest of the poor either, though we would all do well to do so. God might be sending you there, but God might be sending you somewhere else, for need is everywhere. The poor do not have a corner on struggling with demons, and they most certainly are not the only ones who need healing. Everywhere you turn people are fighting for their lives, struggling with all kinds of things from drug abuse to bullying, terminal illness to abandonment, domestic violence to loneliness. You've heard it said before, "everyone has their demons." It's true, and Jesus sends us with his authority to cast them out, to help people be released from them, and experience freedom.

IT'S SCARY TO GO FOR GOD

 ...and he sent them out to proclaim the kingdom of God and to heal the sick.

— LUKE 9:2

We have the Great Commission at the end of the Gospel of Matthew just before Jesus ascends to heaven, but we also have a few other times in Scripture where Jesus sends his disciples as an extension of his ministry. I wonder sometimes about the term "the Great Commission," as if these other commissions are somehow not as great. Perhaps the great part is about the scope. Jesus sends his disciples to the whole world. Here, in the above verse, Jesus just sends his disciples to neighboring towns, but the task itself is still "great"—proclaim the kingdom of God and heal the sick.

I wonder how the disciples felt about all this sending out. Being called is one thing, but being sent is quite another. Being called feels like an honor—you get to be with Jesus! Being called to stand there while he does amazing things is a privilege. Being called to be in the inner circle, seeing others absorb his teaching and have their hearts turned to God, is up-lifting.

Being sent out to do what Jesus does is kind of terrifying.

One of the main reasons it can feel scary is that we never feel adequately prepared. The disciples were in the same boat. They had spent time with Jesus, yes, but where were the actual lessons on how to heal people? Where was the course on how to preach the kingdom of God? Sure, they'd seen it happen, but doing it was an entirely different thing.

We may wonder, like the disciples, about what exactly we are supposed to do when being sent by Jesus. It is to this idea that we turn next.

QUESTIONS FOR REFLECTION OR DISCUSSION

1) Knowing you have authority in Jesus' name, how does this change your perspective about serving?

2) If Jesus is sending you, and he has full authority over everything, what holds you back from going as he asks?

3) Can you relate to the term "Lord" when thinking of Jesus? Is there a term of authority you find more relatable?

4) Brough contends that when Jesus gave his disciples authority over "all demons and to cure diseases" that this was to encourage them to go to those in the greatest need. How does this impact how you see your own Christ-given authority?

5) To what extent is it good to be prepared? When can the desire for preparedness inhibit God's work?

PART III
BE A MAKER

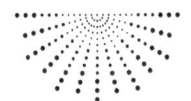

5

MAKE WHAT?

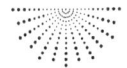

MAKE DISCIPLES

JESUS BEGINS GETTING INTO SPECIFICS. It's not enough to simply go for God without any real idea of what you are going to do. At the same time, it's not as though you will know every detail surrounding your specific commission from God. Your calling will be unique to you but will also trend in the same direction as every other follower of Jesus.

Each of us has the same commission lived out in a different set of circumstances. That commission is to make disciples.

It is usual to object to this very specific mission. Surely "making disciples" cannot be every Christian's job. Perhaps this instruction from Jesus was intended only for the eleven and their successors (e.g. pastors, evangelists, people with some special gift). Perhaps the story of the

Great Commission is only a model for how God sends certain people to do certain things. Surely just *some* people are sent to make disciples and others are sent to do other things, like being doctors, teachers, electricians, or investment bankers.

In some ways, these sentiments are true. God does indeed place people in certain jobs in certain places, but the particular commission of his followers is not to dentistry, or the civil service, or farming, but to something that takes place regardless of the context. God does call to particular jobs, and to family, and to communities, but there is a common commission for all followers of Jesus in all spheres of life, and that common commission is to make disciples.

When we protest against the specifics of this commission, we are really protesting against it being our responsibility. "Surely I am just called to be the best, most ethical and loving lawyer I can be," we might say. But that's it. We go no further. We don't take responsibility for others and especially don't take responsibility for their relationship or potential relationship with Jesus.

We treat connecting others to Jesus the same way we do when recommending a great restaurant to someone. It is certainly not our responsibility—the restaurant owner didn't commission us to go out and tell anyone about our experience. Instead it comes down to whether we enjoyed the food and think our friends will enjoy it, too. If so, we tell them about it. We may even invite them along with us to enjoy the restaurant together.

But following Jesus is quite different than enjoying a

good meal. The one with all authority has commissioned you. Still, we wonder if maybe Jesus has not commissioned "me," but only other people, like pastors.

When Jesus gave this job to the eleven, he was giving the job to the Church. We might still have all kinds of hang-ups about what it actually means to "make disciples" and perhaps even bigger hang-ups about the way the Church in an age of colonialism has gone about this commission. But one thing we must grasp: if we agree that this commission is indeed intended for the Church, then that means Jesus-followers bear individual responsibility for it. If disciple-making was given as a task to the Church, that means it is to be carried out by every person who follows Jesus.

We may not agree with this right away and might even cringe at thinking that one of the Church's primary goals is to "make disciples." Partly it is because we have an institution, or even worse, a building, in mind when we think of the Church. There are real dangers with disciple-making being an institutional mandate. We objectify people on all sides, especially when we come at this from an industrial modernist mindset.

Here is what this thinking looks like... Some people are workers in the factory, and they make (produce) products. That is the goal. We make stuff, and when we make the right things in the right ways, we get rewarded. When we take this thinking into disciple-making, the results are horrific. People are not products or projects, nor are they to be minimized or objectified to be only workers.

Sometimes, however, we treat the mission of the

Church this way. We create systems and processes for people to "plug into" in order for us to carry out the overall goal of producing the thing that we have been told to produce—disciples. Yuck! That sounds so far from what Jesus was really all about.

When Jesus walked around on the earth, meeting people, teaching them about loving their neighbors and (yes!) even loving their enemies, healing people, touching lepers, eating with poor outcasts and rich outcasts too, he didn't seem to be trying to "program" people or make them be anything other than the true human beings that God had created them to be.

It is telling that God became a human being. If we were meant to have an assembly line of disciple-makers churning out disciples, then God (the owner of the disciple-making factory?) would never have joined us on the line. In fact, Jesus always seemed to be outside the factory, outside the confines of the establishment.

So, what does it mean for us to be sent to "make disciples?" Is this a useful term at all?

Maybe it isn't useful anymore. Maybe our English Bible translations and our understanding of them are too conditioned by a western worldview that has for the last several centuries been defined by the Industrial Revolution. Maybe our obsession with production, efficiency, factories, and profits have so colored our way of thinking that we loved the idea of "making disciples" and never really stopped to think about how we actually hear and understand that term.

The King James Version translates the opening of the

Great Commission as "Go ye therefore, and teach all nations…" The basic idea embedded in the commission is that there is an education on offer. When we delve into what the words of this sentence actually mean, it turns out that "teach all nations," isn't quite right either. The word "teach" in the King James, which is "make disciples" in modern translations, is actually closer to "enrol as students."

This is less like making some kind of cookie-cutter Christian from the factory of disciple-makers. It is far more as if Jesus had been running a private school for his closest followers, and then he says, "Enrolment is open. Spread the word. Anyone, from any culture, in any place, can have equal access to me to come and learn."

When Jesus commissions his followers, he is not primarily commissioning an institution or a set of programs. Something that is a church responsibility is really a responsibility of each person in the Church. Programs, institutions, and buildings are meant to provide support for the mission of the Church.

This becomes a little more clear in the context of Christian families. Many Christian parents behave as though bringing their kids to Church two or three times a month will provide the "Christian education" their children require. But it doesn't take much working out to realize that children will learn far more about being a disciple of Jesus from their parents than from anywhere else. Here, disciple-making is the primary responsibility of the parents. Programs, buildings, and institutions can never play much more than a supporting role.

This is, in fact, how it is for most people—not just parents with their children. The primary disciple-makers are the existing disciples. If you have read this far, I hope you know that this is you!

WHAT ABOUT SOCIAL MINISTRY?

Does the Church do more than making disciples? Of course, but it ought not do less than making disciples. Sadly, disciple-making has been put on the back burner in many corners of Christian life. This has been done at times in favor of "real" mission work such as supporting the poor through social programs and the like. It is no small tragedy that making disciples has for many churches not been seen as part of mission, and mission has ended up synonymous with raising money for social, development, and relief work, as important as these are.

The reverse is also true in some corners of the Church —at times disciple-making has been so over-emphasized that it has supplanted social programs. Or worse, we made receiving the benefits of social programs contingent on hearing a discipleship message. More bluntly, there are organizations that require the hungry at a soup kitchen to listen to a sermon before they are allowed to have a meal, as though the right to food is contingent on the potential of a disciple being made. This should never be and is so far from Jesus' call to love of neighbor.

The dichotomy between discipleship ministries and social ministries is a false one. Jesus called us to feed the hungry, and he called us to make disciples. As Jesus conducted his ministry, continued by the apostles, we find that they did both things regularly, usually with the same groups of people. It wasn't that the hungry were one group, and there was another group who were invited to discipleship. They were the same people!

1) How do you respond to the idea that all followers of Jesus have the same commission, to make disciples, lived out in a different set of circumstances?

2) How do you understand disciple-making? Have you heard this always connected to the programs of the institutional Church?

3) How would you understand "enrolment is open?" Is this different than "make disciples?"

4) Brough writes: "Programs, institutions, and buildings are meant to provide support for the mission of the Church." Where do you see this actually taking place? Do you ever see an over-emphasis on "programs" of the Church, rather than the Church being the people and institutions playing supportive roles?

5) Do you see a certain kind of ministry being over-emphasized? What could you do to address areas of ministry that might be overlooked?

6) What opportunities do you have to serve others? Are there ways to see disciple-making as central to this service?

6

WALKING ON SOMEONE ELSE'S TURF

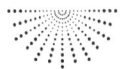

POWER REVISITED

> But you will receive power when the Holy Spirit has come upon you; and you will be my witnesses in Jerusalem, in all Judea and Samaria, and to the ends of the earth.' When he had said this, as they were watching, he was lifted up, and a cloud took him out of their sight. While he was going and they were gazing up towards heaven, suddenly two men in white robes stood by them. They said, 'Men of Galilee, why do you stand looking up towards heaven? This Jesus, who has been taken up from you into heaven, will come in the same way as you saw him go into heaven.'

— ACTS 1:8-11

The book of Acts begins in a time of waiting. Just before going into heaven to take his place at the right hand of the Father, Jesus talks about the coming of the Holy Spirit. "You will receive power when the Holy Spirit has come upon you," he says.

Already, in the gospels, we have seen power and authority conferred upon the disciples. It will happen again in the giving of the Spirit. In reading over the book of Acts, we find that the Spirit and the Spirit's power never leaves the apostles and is very much present in the life of every new believer.

In fact, the Holy Spirit could be seen as the primary actor in the book of Acts. I sometimes think that perhaps the book of Acts ought to be called "The Acts of the Holy Spirit" rather than "The Acts of the Apostles." It is the Spirit that drives the ministry and mission of the newly forming Church. The Spirit sparks a movement, using people and communities, powerfully transforming lives.

Jesus' promise before he ascends to heaven is that his followers will receive power. While this is clearly pointing to the specific moment described in Acts 2 when the Holy Spirit shows up on the day of Pentecost, the receiving of power and the Spirit can and ought to be claimed by all Jesus-followers. With the Holy Spirit, you have been given the power to go! Because of the Spirit, you are able to carry out the mission that God has placed before you.

We are called to be bold in pointing people to Jesus,

but how we do that is so important. The power we have been given is not to coerce people into believing in Jesus.

The kind of power we have been given is exemplified in the power Jesus wielded. Jesus was a King who washed the feet of his followers. Jesus ate with outcasts. Jesus touched the unclean and diseased. Jesus acted powerfully, but, as you well know, it was never to "convert" in the sleazy, salesy, bait-and-switch sense or force something on people in a turn-or-burn sense. Yes, people were changed when they encountered Jesus, but their "conversions" flowed from an encounter based on his love, which was always offered prior to any faith claims being made by the people. Or as the Apostle Paul put it: "But God proves his love for us in that, *while we still were sinners,* Christ died for us" (Romans 5:8).

Jesus seemed to reserve his harshest critique, particularly his theological critique, for those who were part of the religious establishment of the day. The Pharisees were Jesus' greatest opponents, and they represent orthodoxy. It is far too easy for Christians to claim that the Pharisees represent the *Jewish* establishment, and that Jesus was starting something new. We are tempted to uncritically claim that we belong to the new covenant, the Church, and that we always stand with Jesus, but we must look honestly at ourselves and the history of the Church.

There has been much claiming of power by the Church over the centuries, and often that power has been accompanied by theologies and actions of domination over others. Yet our founder displayed his power in serving the sinner, the outcast, and the ones considered unclean.

When people outside the Church take a look at the behavior of the Church, they often see problems, scandals, or what they perceive as pointless theological arguing. Sadly, scandal and theological backbiting are indeed ever-present realities, but don't get me wrong—I am not down on the Church. The Church is the Body of Christ—it really is! When we only see the arguments, the frustrations, the abuses of power, we miss that much of the Church (I would argue most of it) is still miraculously focused around the care of others because of the abiding presence of the Spirit of Jesus, who laid down his life for the sake of the world.

It may not always seem like that to you, but we can tend not to see how much Christians are doing to love their neighbors. We can often forget about the hospital visits, the walking with people through grief, the sharing of a meal, the mid-week program for kids, the connections with a local school, the soup kitchen, the food bank, the additional social assistance, the advocacy, the support of relief work around the world. The Church is doing a ton to serve in Jesus' name.

Still, we can also behave as Pharisees, often because we don't want to give up power or allow our human power to be replaced by the true power of the Holy Spirit, which is always the self-emptying power that Jesus put on display for us. For all the good we do, Christians can also keep the outcast at arm's-length. We support theologies that continue oppression and discrimination. We argue about theology, morality, and politics, forgetting that we hurt real people in the process.

A strange tension exists in the life of the Church, and perhaps in the lives of most Christians. Are we really standing with Jesus, or are we acting against him as people more concerned about our own power, morality, or politics?

We have great power. It is given by the Spirit of God. How can we use it in ways that are in line with Jesus, as we are sent out to serve others?

ALL THE WAY TO THE ENDS OF THE EARTH

The Great Commission speaks of the disciples going to all the nations. The commissioning at Jesus's ascension talks about going to the ends of the earth. You certainly can't rule out that God may be sending you to places far from home. But please do not ignore the reality that Jesus names other places before the ends of the earth: "Jerusalem, Judea, and Samaria."

We are sent first to the places we inhabit. We may think of our city or town, or even our neighborhood. We may think even smaller: our family, our household, our job, our school. What does it look like to make disciples in these contexts?

I do not believe that it looks like endlessly talking about Jesus and how people need to accept him right away. As I'm sure you know, this will more than likely turn people away from you and from anything you have to say. This isn't just "poor evangelism technique." It also looks nothing like what Jesus or his first followers did.

Certainly talking about Jesus is important, but attention must be paid to the right moment for it. Often, you will sense those moments. A conversation at work will take a turn, and you'll sense that talking about your relationship with God is the right thing to do. Or you will have a feeling that you need to offer to pray for someone. You might be scared to take the step and offer your own faith story or offer to pray for an individual, but if you are a follower of Jesus, you will get feelings in conversations that push you in your heart and mind to speak. Make no mistake, this can be pretty daunting.

I have had many such moments in my life. Sadly, I usually recognize them most readily after I've let them pass by. A moment opens up in a conversation where it has turned toward God, or some matter related to the meaning of life or spirituality, and I've let it slip by without saying much of anything. I encourage you to seize the opportunity to point others to Jesus when the opportunity arises.

Jesus sending his followers to the ends of the earth is all about opportunity. He will provide his followers with plenty of moments to act and to speak. They will be able to go all the way to the ends of the earth, and people will respond to hearing about Jesus. This is still true. Many of us in North America and Europe don't feel as though this is the case, but Christianity is growing on a global scale. All the time, all over the world, people are hearing about Jesus for the first time, and are turning to follow him.

You are asked to speak up as the opportunity arises, but what about as you wait for opportunities? That is actually the majority of the time. What is the correct posture or way of being in between the moments of talking about Jesus?

My simple answer is love. We have a Great Commission and a Great Commandment. Love the Lord your God, and love your neighbor as yourself. Treat others well. Go out of your way to extend caring to others. Serve people in your family, in your school, in your workplace. Treat everyone with respect, and show no partiality. Do this for those you know well (those you like and those you dislike) and for people you pass on the street. Treat everyone with dignity. They are all children of God.

A disposition of love, kindness, caring is the disposition of a follower of Jesus. Take a hard look at yourself, and ask whether you are living a loving life. Where are you acting in ways that are judgmental or critical? When are you self-righteous or self-centered? When are you simply hurtful to others? These are the moments to repent. Are you someone who complains about how others need to change their ways? Look in the mirror, and find grace.

A famous misquote of St. Francis of Assisi is "Preach the Gospel at all times. Use words if necessary." Maybe you didn't know that St. Francis never said anything of the sort. In fact, St. Francis was known as a great preacher in his time. Many people love this saying because it means we can focus solely on our loving actions to draw people to Christ. The problem with the quote is that it sets up a false dichotomy between our words and actions.

I wouldn't want you to read that in my writing. I am not trying to say that you should never say anything about Jesus and should only focus on loving actions. I believe your actions and words are meant to work together. In living a life of other-centered love, opportunities to tell people about the source of that love will arise. You must be on the lookout, and be ready to share your story.

You can also create your own opportunities for speaking about Jesus. I have a friend who chose to get to know his immediate neighbors on his street better. They became good friends. Over time, in their conversations, he began to sense a deeper longing among them and invited them to his house for a meal and to honestly talk about life. In the course of the conversations, God, Jesus, and Spirituality came up. Eventually, they became a house church, and several other house churches started up as a result of that first one.

I have been surprised where my words have reached once I embraced writing as part of my life. While my books haven't been read too widely, there are people in a number of different countries who have read them. I have heard from readers about the blessing of my words. In some cases, something I've written or an interview I have conducted for a podcast has sparked a conversation with someone about spiritual matters.

Not everyone will start a house Church, or write a book, or produce a podcast, but these examples point to the reality that you don't have to wait for opportunities.

Made in the image of the ever-creative God, you can create them.

The way to create opportunities is through examining your gifts. If you love to write, then maybe writing a blog, or even posting really thoughtful and loving words on social media are a way to open up opportunity (as a refreshing contrast with the many words written online that tear people down!) Maybe writing isn't your thing. Maybe, it is baking. What if you started baking for the people on your street? Maybe your thing is having great barbecues in your backyard. What if you invited some people who aren't in your normal circle?

The examples could go on forever, but the principle is the same no matter what. What is your gift, and how might it be given in service to others—not just within the Church, but in your life? And then, be ready because the offering of your gift in love may just help someone be open to hearing about the source of love, a love that will not let them go.

The amazing thing about the world today is that we are not limited by space anymore. The ends of the earth are not so far away as they used to be. Begin where you are, and see where Jesus will take you.

OF ALL NATIONS

When Jesus commands his followers to make disciples "of all nations," I immediately have some pause. Perhaps it is that I am Canadian, and we are a multi-cultural nation. Probably every nation in the world is represented in the approximately seven hundred thousand people living in my hometown of Winnipeg.

I have pause not simply out of respect for other cultures, but also because of our poor track record in disciple-making cross-culturally. "All nations" immediately makes me think of the term "First Nations," one of the terms referring to Indigenous peoples in Canada, acknowledging that their nations were the first in this land.

European nations came to North America and did terrible harm to Indigenous peoples. Remarkably, there are numerous Indigenous people who follow Jesus despite years of abuse at the hands of Church and government. Many Indigenous people who are Christian seek to maintain or reclaim the traditional ways of their people. Some Christians balk at this, believing that the traditional ways, with their spiritual roots, are incompatible with Christianity. However, we rarely stop to evaluate if what we do in our churches is compatible with the true heart of Christianity.

This brings up an important point about the methodology of disciple-making. We must learn from the errors/terrors of the past. We must acknowledge that while Christ was shared, it was often done in conjunction with terrible abuse and pain. Christ was shared and continues to be shared with massive cultural assumptions of what it means to follow Jesus. It is a testament to the strength of Indigenous peoples that there have been steps toward healing in recent years, though there is still so much more to be done.

What can we learn from the past, and specifically from the way in which mission, sending, and disciple-making were conducted in the colonial world?

I believe it would be a mistake to decide that so much damage was done in the name of Christ that now we are not going to "go." Not going at all is usually less about not wanting to do further damage, and much more about fear. We don't want to go because it is complicated or difficult. We don't want to be seen as forcing a certain Christian agenda upon people.

If you are someone who feels this, then you may actually be a good person to go in the name of Christ. We don't need any missionaries that believe their job is to "bring Christ to those lost people who need our version of Christianity." We need those who know that pointing people to Christ must be done in a loving and humble way, with no sense of superiority, and with no hidden agenda.

This is difficult to pull off in today's multi-cultural and pluralistic world. But this is what Christ calls us to. We are sent to today's world—not to an idealized version of the past.

So, how do we make disciples of all nations?

The single best way to move forward is to learn from how Jesus interacted with people. Beyond that, we listen (allow ourselves to be witnessed to), and then we act as witnesses ourselves, pointing people to Jesus through our own stories.

QUESTIONS FOR REFLECTION OR DISCUSSION

1) How do you feel about the idea that you have power from the Holy Spirit to "go"?

2) When you look at the way that Jesus served others, how does this affect your understanding of the kind of power we are given? Can you think of examples of people who wielded the kind of power on display in the King who washed the feet of his followers, ate with outcasts, and touched the unclean and diseased?

3) Have you ever sensed it was the right time to talk about God or Jesus? What did you do?

4) What are some of the ways you see people living out a disposition of love, kindness, and caring?

5) What are some of the ways you can create opportunities or occasions for conversations about God,

deepening relationships, or disciple-making? What gifts do you have to offer to others that might lead to these opportunities?

6) In thinking about sharing your faith, is there a way to be both bold and humble? How so?

PART IV
RECLAIMING WITNESSING

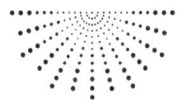

7

YOU ARE A WITNESS

TEACHING OBEDIENCE (CRINGE)

> …and teaching them to obey everything that I have commanded you.
>
> — MATTHEW 28:20

JESUS COMMISSIONS us to go out, make disciples, and teach them to obey. On the surface this seems arrogant or triumphalist: we have the right answers, and we will teach the people who don't understand the right way to live. Beyond this, we also have a general dislike for the concept of obedience.

But the idea of obedience to Jesus must be read in light of the rest of the gospel of Matthew and really in light of the rest of the Bible. Jesus does not ask for his disciples to teach obedience to the Church. He asks them to teach obedience to everything Jesus commanded them.

Our problem with obedience usually stems from assumptions that we make about what it means to be obedient to Jesus. We too quickly equate this obedience with "being a good Christian," which translates into all kinds of rules and regulations about spiritual and moral behavior. We think Jesus is sending us out to make clone Christians, but disciples are so far removed from this idea. We must take a close look at the content of Jesus' teaching. Only then can we have a sense for why teaching all people to obey what he taught it is so important and life-giving.

Our fundamental assumption about obedience to Jesus ought to be that Jesus wants us to obey him for our sakes —that is for the sake of all of us, for the common good for all people.

In Matthew's gospel, Jesus is recorded as doing a lot of teaching. His most famous teaching, the Sermon on the Mount, is found here. This is the teaching that begins with "Blessed are the poor in spirit, for theirs is the kingdom of heaven" (Matthew 5:3). As soon as we read the Beatitudes (the opening of the Sermon on the Mount), we are taken into the world of Jesus, where the grieving are comforted, the meek inherit the earth, those who hunger for justice are filled, the merciful receive mercy, the pure in heart meet God face to face, and the peacemakers are cherished as God's own children.

Much of Jesus' teaching is challenging (e.g., his teaching on divorce in Matthew 5:31-32). We ought to wrestle with his teaching, be convicted by it, spend a lifetime interpreting it. Jesus' teaching needs to work on us over many years. Yet, much of his teaching, even with just a cursory reading, is so obviously life-transforming. Jesus' teaching is good. I don't say this to be trite. I mean this more in the sense of when God looked at creation each day and called it good.

Our issue with teaching people to obey is that obedience somehow seems wrong in a culture that so values individual freedom. Yet, Jesus' teaching is all about the good life for all. The "good life" is not about getting everything you desire. This isn't a health and wealth prosperity gospel. No, this good life is about truly being a better person that goes on to make the world around you better as well. Jesus' teaching is about each person flourishing in freedom in relation to each other. It isn't about just your own freedom, but about everyone's freedom.

The following gems are just from this one sermon that Jesus delivered on the hillside:

"If anyone strikes you on the right cheek, turn the other also; and if anyone wants to sue you and take your coat, give your cloak as well" (Matthew 5:39-40).

"Give to everyone who begs from you, and do not refuse anyone who wants to borrow from you" (Matthew 5:42).

"Love your enemies and pray for those who persecute you" (Matthew 5:44).

"No one can serve two masters; for a slave will either hate the one and love the other, or be devoted to the one and despise the other. You cannot serve God and wealth" (Matthew 6:24).

"And can any of you by worrying add a single hour to your span of life?... If God so clothes the grass of the field, which is alive today and tomorrow is thrown into the oven, will he not much more clothe you" (Matthew 6:27,30)?

"Do not judge, so that you may not be judged" (Matthew 7:1).

"In everything do to others as you would have them do to you" (Matthew 7:12).

This is all in just one sermon!

Of course, if you are reading this book you are probably already convinced about the goodness and transformative power of Jesus' teaching. More than likely, you wish you held more closely to his teaching yourself. Instructing others in obeying Jesus is often another story, however. We will usually bounce between two extremes when it comes to inviting others to obey Jesus.

1) We are hesitant because we don't think we should be forcing religion on anyone.

2) We are overly enthusiastic and end up forcing our own understanding or our own version of religion on people.

It is not that we need to find a middle ground between these two. Rather, the same antidote is needed in both scenarios. We must focus on several things. First, we focus on the person to whom we have been sent. We focus on them as a person. They are another human being, not a project we are working on. Second, we focus on Jesus and his teaching.

The mistake we make in both extreme cases is that we are overly focused on the conversion or transformation of the person. We come to the person with a goal of making them into a disciple rather than simply having a relationship with them as a human being. This leads to something quite unhealthy. We begin forcing religion, or we begin trying to force a conversion.

When our top-of-mind goal is working toward the conversion of individuals, we have turned people into projects and have turned Jesus, his teaching, and the gospel, into a tool. Why does it make such a difference to move away from focusing on conversion? And hasn't Jesus sent us to make disciples? Isn't that the whole point of this book?

In essence, we are removing ourselves from the conversion equation and leaving that to the Holy Spirit. The question around teaching people obedience to Jesus is essentially the same as asking "How do we make disciples?" While it will look different in different contexts, the answer is not about conversion. It is more basic than that. The basic answer is: We point people to Jesus.

WITNESSES

> …you will be my witnesses…

— ACTS 1:8

The fundamental posture of the Christian is to be a witness, though I think we have lost what that word means. When set in a religious context, we get all hung up on this word. It conjures images of door-to-door evangelists (another word we probably ought to reclaim!). I always think of someone with a very specific agenda. "Witnessing" feels to me like it is about convincing—as though it is all about talking someone into something when they don't want to be talked into it. The door-to-door evangelist is essentially the door-to-door salesperson, and the product is Jesus.

Maybe this is the reason so many people have adverse reactions to the words "witness" and "evangelism." In many places in the world, the unexpected visitor is a welcome guest, but in western culture, they are an intrusion. I don't want anyone showing up on my doorstep trying to sell something to me or convince me of anything. I'm at home to enjoy being at home.

So let's take this word "witness" out of its religious context, and put it in the place where it is much more familiar—the courtroom. In the courtroom, "witness" is not a particularly distressing term.

Think for a moment what a witness in a courtroom really does. At the most basic level, they tell about what they have seen and experienced, and they swear to tell "the truth, the whole truth, and nothing but the truth." They must answer questions and do so to the best of their ability.

Sometimes there are expert witnesses that are put on the stand because they have some kind of knowledge or skill in a particular field. Other times, witnesses are just regular people who happen to have been at the right place at the right time (or the wrong place at the wrong time, depending on how you see it).

Now, let's apply this basic understanding of "witness" to Jesus sending his disciples into the world. "You will be my witnesses," he says. Those first disciples were to tell about what they had seen and experienced. They were to not shy away from the truth. In fact, the heart of their "witnessing" was pretty simple: Jesus is risen from the dead. This was the absolute truth that they knew because they had seen it.

The advantage for the first disciples was that they were taking the news of Jesus' resurrection into a world that had never heard it before. Someone had risen from the dead, and they were eyewitnesses.

We cannot claim that we are witnesses in the same way as those first disciples. We are two millennia away from having physically seen the resurrection of Jesus. We will certainly encounter many people who do not believe in the resurrection of Jesus, and our talking about it as a fact won't convince them. We are not eyewitnesses to it.

Today, people aren't really asking questions about Jesus' resurrection, though certainly its historicity is widely doubted because it doesn't seem plausible. A more central question for today's doubter, however, is that if Jesus did actually rise from the dead, why would that matter? If Jesus really is risen, so what? Why would anyone choose to believe this?

At the heart of the early gospel was something else

besides the basic fact of the resurrection. The claim that Jesus was risen from the dead was the content of their "witnessing," but they also claimed that Jesus was Lord. This claim is much less about sharing what they had seen and much more about their reflection on the difference Jesus makes.

If Jesus is Lord, it means that no one else is. It means that only Jesus is in charge. In the first century, this meant that the Roman Emperor was not the ultimate authority. If you remember, Pilate presented Jesus to the people saying, "Here is your king," and the crowd chanted, "We have no king but the Emperor."

The early witnesses told the story of resurrection as a story of vindication. If Jesus was risen, then he truly was Lord over everything—even over life and death themselves.

How does any of this affect how we understand ourselves as witnesses?

A WITNESS WHO LISTENS

> Let the same mind be in you that was in Christ Jesus, who, though he was in the form of God, did not regard equality with God as something to be exploited, but emptied himself, taking the form of a slave, being born in human likeness.
>
> — PHILIPPIANS 2:6-7

Being ready to share your own story of the risen Jesus is at the heart of being a witness, but there is something more fundamental. What I wish to suggest may seem like a bit of a leap, and maybe it is, but think of this flowing from the very nature of God.

The Christian faith is full of paradox. It is a faith centered on Jesus after all, and the deepest paradoxes of all are found in the person of Christ. The boundless and everlasting one limits himself by becoming human. The immortal one gives himself over to death. The sinless one receives the punishment of a criminal. The king becomes a servant, bending low to wash the feet of his followers.

It turns out that our best way of being a witness is also, in a way, paradoxical. We are sent as witnesses whose first actions are not to speak, but to listen.

Yes, there are times to proclaim Christ loudly and proudly, but when we do this as our very first step, we are entering dangerous territory. Are we proclaiming from on high, dictating to someone how they must be, what they must accept, and how they must behave? If we are, we must measure this against what Jesus himself did.

Jesus's way of being a sent one was to completely identify with those to whom he was sent. His first action was not speaking, it was the incarnation: God in flesh, or on the basic level, simply being human, and therefore being in relationship. The Message translation of John 1:14 says it like this, "The Word became flesh and blood, and moved into the neighborhood."

Jesus is present with people from the beginning of his story, but his actual ministry didn't begin until he was about thirty years old. What was he doing for those first thirty years? Why wasn't he urgently racing around sharing his message? Was he just too busy being a carpenter?

Obviously, we can't know why Jesus waited, but the fact that he did wait tells us something. Being present, being human, living life, being "in the neighborhood" is vastly important. Understanding our surroundings, being in the world as Jesus was in the world is a must. Jesus' ministry was based around a strong proclamation that the Kingdom of God was near, but he waited before he started speaking. I would argue that he listened before he witnessed.

We don't listen only in order to know how to say the most persuasive words when it is our turn to speak. It isn't about gaining just enough trust to be listened to. Listening to the other in the way you witness to Jesus is not a trick or a technique. Real listening is at the heart of human relationships. It gives honor and respect to the other person. It provides a way to true mutuality in your relationship. You recognize the other, even when they seem so very different from yourself, as someone beautiful and good, made in the image of God.

YOUR OWN STORY TO TELL

We must point to what we have seen and experienced in the same way that the early disciples did. Being a witness is not running off a set script. It is telling your own story of God at work in your life. Where have you encountered

Jesus? Describe those moments, and point to the reality that he is Lord.

I have run across many people who believe that the story of Jesus in their own life is not a particularly good story. They downplay it. I think this is because they have heard other stories of complete turn-around or miracle, and theirs doesn't seem to measure up. They don't have stories about addictions that have been broken by Jesus, or getting out of abusive situations, or having some kind of miraculous healing. I know so many faithful people who feel they can't tell their story because there doesn't seem much to tell.

If this is you, please dig deeper and really think about where Jesus has been most active in your life. Your story is important, and you too are a witness.

My own story could be told in this way…

I grew up in the Church. My family always went to church, so I always knew about Jesus. In my teenage years, I went to a youth group and it had a big impact on me. Eventually, I felt called to ministry, and I became a pastor.

This is not a very compelling story. And where is the active presence of the Risen Jesus in this story?

Instead, I might want to tell just a little more about those teenage years. I had always gone to church, but in my teenage years and early twenties, I really felt my entire life come alive. I remember going to a particular worship service with a group of friends, and I honestly can't remember much about it. I do remember that I felt something like I had never felt before. The message that night clearly laid out that Jesus' death was important, and that, through his death, I was somehow rescued from my sin. This may not sound like a big deal, but I felt guilty a lot of the time, and in that moment, I felt freedom from it all. I learned as I got older that Jesus is someone who sets you free, not just from guilt, but from anything that might be holding you back or weighing you down.

What is crazy about that night is that I had actually heard about all of it before. It just hadn't sunk in very deep until then. That was one of the first times that I really knew Jesus was more than what is contained in the Bible. Jesus showed up that night and, in some way that I still can't explain, I met him.

This is a better story than just glossing over the details. When I tell this story, I'm witnessing, but it would be so much easier for me to just make this story into not that big of a deal. In the end, it was just a worship service, and I remember so few of the details. But the thing is: that night was a big deal for me. It is my story, and it is meaningful to me. That is what will make it meaningful for someone who knows me.

Be ready to share your own story of the Risen Jesus. This is what it means to be a witness.

REFLECTION ON THE MAN BORN BLIND

In John 9, we read of a man who had been blind from birth. Jesus heals him in a very particular and peculiar way. He makes mud by spitting on some dirt and then spreads the mud on the man's eyes, telling him to go and wash it off in the pool of Siloam. We are clued in that

LET GOD SEND

something far more is about to happen in this story, when it is explained that the word Siloam means "sent."

The man does what Jesus tells him and can see again, but when he returns, Jesus is gone. This healing creates a stir in the community with people not believing that the newly sighted man is the same man that used to sit and beg.

Of course, the townspeople bring the man to the Pharisees since they are the community leaders, and that is when we find out the real problem everyone is having.

> Now it was a sabbath day when Jesus made the mud and opened his eyes.
>
> — JOHN 9:14

Jesus had broken sabbath laws by doing work. The work he did was making mud and healing someone. When the man explains things to the Pharisees, they are divided. Some claim the one who did this healing must be from God, and others claim he is a sinner for Sabbath-breaking. The ones who believe he is from God quickly fade from the story, and soon, a kind of witch-hunt is underway. The Pharisees are after the truth and are after Jesus.

They begin by bringing in the parents of the man who had been blind. They know nothing and tell the Pharisees that their son is of age and they should ask him. This short scene illustrates the kind of trouble the man was in.

His own parents were afraid to say anything or jump to their son's defense.

The Pharisees bring the man who had been blind back in for more questioning. Only, this time, they don't really question him. Instead, they demand that he renounce his healer, and they say that this will bring glory to God. The man refuses to do what they say and what follows is one of the greatest conversations recorded in the Bible.

> So for the second time they called the man who had been blind, and they said to him, 'Give glory to God! We know that this man is a sinner.' He answered, 'I do not know whether he is a sinner. One thing I do know, that though I was blind, now I see.' They said to him, 'What did he do to you? How did he open your eyes?' He answered them, 'I have told you already, and you would not listen. Why do you want to hear it again? Do you also want to become his disciples?'
>
> — JOHN 9:14-27

I just love that last line. Of course the Pharisees don't want to become Jesus' disciples! The man is just being snarky and trying to make his point. He has decided to be a disciple of the one who opened his eyes. The opponents of Jesus are begging for details. "Tell us the story again and this time tell us what really happened. Tell us that this Jesus is a sinner." But the man just says, "I don't know whether he is a sinner. I just know I was blind, but now I see!"

This story can be a bit tricky for Christians to relate to. We immediately want to side with Jesus and with the man born blind. The problem for Christians is that the Pharisees represent the good, upstanding religious people in this story. Jesus is a rule-breaker. The Pharisees, the rule-followers, classify Jesus as a sinner.

God is already acting in the lives of people, changing them, healing them. But what happens when God's activity is outside of the normal religious constructs? Christians may be accustomed to thinking about going to church and then being sent out in order to "spread the gospel" or "to serve in Christ's name." But this story is different. In this story, Jesus has healed a man on the margins and that man becomes a sent-one. He becomes a witness sent not to the world, but to the religious ones. And his message is biting. The one you call a "rule-breaker" is actually the one to follow.

The man born blind points people to Jesus. He witnesses to what God is really up to and, for him, that is a massive risk. In fact, as you follow the story to its completion, you find that he ends up being kicked out of the community. He wants to follow Jesus and is cast out because of it.

Notice again how hard this is to relate to within a worldview that is predominantly Christian. If you are living in a place where Christians are persecuted or where sharing your faith with others could lead to expulsion from your community, then you find solidarity with this man and his story. But what about places where the culture is not overtly hostile to Christianity? What about places where going to church is accepted even if it might be somewhat socially unacceptable to talk about Jesus? And what about places where Christendom is dying, like North America and Western Europe? Where there is a distant (or sometimes not-so-distant) cultural memory of church, but where church and Christianity are increasingly associated with things like legalism and hypocrisy?

The story begins to read quite differently in our current "end of Christendom" context. The man born blind is rejected by his own faith community because he refuses to admit that the one who healed him has broken a religious rule. If we just take this description of the story at face value and couple that with the feeling about church being an organization obsessed with correct rules and doctrine, we find that, in the view of the wider culture, the Church aligns less with Jesus and the man born blind, and far more with the Pharisees. And so, what is God trying to tell us, here?

Will some of us be sent with a message of healing and out-of-bounds grace to Christians obsessed with "correct religion," even at the risk of being cast out?

Others might be sent to those who have other unbendable containers for the way the world works or the way they believe reality is constructed. Some people are religious about their Christianity. Others are religious about their atheism. Still others have a mix of beliefs, or grab from several traditions to build their own spirituality but might be quite hostile to the idea of "organized religion."

Their container that might need breaking is a belief that "all churches are full of hypocrites," or "all Christians are moral prudes."

What does it look like to be sent to the people in our lives who have very set beliefs: whether it is a strict moralism, a strict atheism, a strict anti-religiosity, even a strict pluralism that is overly condemning of more traditional modes of religious belief? The man born blind is actually a great model for us. The Pharisees only had one category for Jesus and everything Jesus represented. "We know this man is a sinner." The man born blind avoids the issue of whether Jesus is a sinner entirely when he says, "I do not know whether he is a sinner. One thing I do know, that though I was blind, now I see." This is a true witness to God at work in the world. We never have it all figured out, but we can point to what God has done in our lives.

Church people are great at arguing about rules, whether it is about sexuality, abortion, gender roles, or immigration, to name the current hot-button issues. Interestingly, it isn't just church people who argue about these things. But in all the arguing, are we listening to the stories of what God is doing in the lives of real people? Are we actually listening to the immigrant or refugee, or someone of the opposite gender, or someone with a different sexual orientation than us? The question here is how can you be less like the Pharisees and actually allow yourself to be impacted in compassion by someone else's story? Because it is quite possible that God is sending someone to you and not just sending you to someone.

Equally, what is your own story? To whom are you

sent? When someone questions you or interrogates you, how do you respond? When you end up in an argument about religion and someone is being judgmental about how "all Christians are judgmental," what do you say? Maybe, you can take a cue from the man born blind. "I don't know whether all Christians are judgmental (maybe all people are!), but one thing I do know..." And then tell them, honestly, about the change that has happened in your life because of the grace of God in Jesus Christ.

And if anyone keeps pushing you, then maybe you'll have the opportunity to echo the former blind man and say, "Why do you keep asking me all this? Is it because you too want to be a follower of Jesus?"

QUESTIONS FOR REFLECTION OR DISCUSSION

1) How do you respond to the idea of teaching people to obey Jesus' teaching?

2) Brough writes: "Jesus' teaching is about each person flourishing in freedom in relation to each other. It isn't about just your own freedom, but about everyone's freedom." How might our pursuit of personal freedom get in the way of our obedience to Jesus? How might it get in the way of allowing others to flourish or truly be free?

3) How would you respond to someone if they asked why Jesus matters or why his resurrection matters?

4) Do you have any negative associations with the word "witness?"

5) How does the incarnation as Jesus' first activity inform our way of being witnesses?

6) Take some moment to think about your own story of the Risen Jesus in your life. Remember the details. How would you tell your story without downplaying it? You may want to take time to write it down, or if you are studying with a group, split up into small groups of two or three to really listen to one another's stories.

8

LISTENING, SEEING, TELLING

PLACE OF HOPE

From time to time, I have the joyful opportunity to worship with the people at Place of Hope Indigenous Presbyterian Church. The congregation is made up of more than ninety percent Indigenous people, almost all of them living in deep poverty. They gather on Sunday afternoons for worship and a meal, packing into a space too small for their growing community. Half of the congregation are children.

The worship service begins with a smudge. Smudging is a practice common among numerous Indigenous peoples in North America. It usually involves burning tobacco, sweetgrass, sage, or cedar in a bowl. At Place of Hope, the minister brings the bowl around to each person and, if they choose, they can make a motion with their hand bringing the smudge towards them, often over their head, along their arms and hands, and toward their heart.

The smudge is a practice focused on healing or cleansing. I have seen smudging done before in more solemn assemblies, but at Place of Hope, things are a little more chaotic. I did mention half the congregation are children. There are crying or gurgling babies, people coming and going, and there are elders, youth, and also some non-indigenous people receiving healing as the smudge passes over them.

After the smudge, the worship continues with two songs as an eagle staff is brought in and put at the front of the room. The staff traditionally represents and honors certain tribes and has emblems with the four colors representing the four races of earth, acknowledging the value of all peoples of the world.

The songs they sing at the beginning are simple songs of praise which, when I attended for the first time, was my first point of familiarity. Every week they sing "Lord, I Lift Your Name on High" and "Awesome God." They do actions. The kids participate. They do the same two songs, songs which I am pretty sick of hearing, to be honest, from my youth ministry days in the 1990s. But kids need repetition, and they can all join in. The kids don't need to be told to come to the front as the songs play. They just come.

A spiral-bound notebook is passed around to the adults in the congregation for people to write their prayer requests. The children join hands, and the minister prays a short prayer. Then they share the love of Jesus around the circle. This is done by them squeezing the hand of the next person in the circle. They watch as the love of Jesus is passed from person to person. This takes a while as sometimes the youngest among them need some help to remind them to pass it on. The leaders make sure every child receives the love of Jesus and every child passes it on. This is what they are supposed to do out there in their lives, they are told.

The children leave to go to Sunday school, and the prayer requests from the notebook are read out and prayed for. Every time I have been there, there is tragedy and death that has touched the community. We pray for suicides, gang violence, overdoses, abuse, housing problems like water pipes freezing in the winter and landlords doing nothing. The list is heartbreaking. They pray. There is some singing in Ojibway, Cree, and in English. Old gospel hymns seem to be a favorite. There is a sermon, and every sermon I've heard at Place of Hope addresses the reality of the people's lives. It is an acknowledgement of the injustice that they live each day, but it is also an offering of hope. Babies continue to cry during the sermon. No one bats an eye at this. All are welcome, no matter the noise.

The most striking thing to me about worshipping with this congregation is not the Indigenous traditional practices in which they participate, though these are beautiful and meaningful for the community. It is their reliance and focus on Jesus Christ. They witness to Jesus as they worship. Each element of what they do is an expression of who they are as a people, and at the center of it all is Jesus.

When I worship at Place of Hope, I am reminded that the way this community follows Jesus is not the way I follow Jesus. Part of this community's way of following Jesus is to honor all races and peoples right at the start. They do that with the symbol of the eagle staff. Part of this community's way of following Jesus is for each individual to have the option to receive cleansing and healing through the practice of smudging. Those practices are not my practices.

Some might worry about Indigenous spirituality mixing with Christian spirituality, even though Christian spirituality has been mixing with all kinds of other spiritualities for centuries. We might do better to worry more about the unholy mixing of "Christian living" and consumerism than about whether a particular spiritual practice is "Christian enough" in a community that is not our own.

Western and Northern Christianity is bound up with modernist ways of evaluation and judgment. I immediately turn to evaluating whether something is "right" or not. Instead, through practice, I have come to learn to resist the urge to evaluate or judge. I am not in the place to do that. It is tempting to say that Christ will be the judge, and in the grand scheme of things, this is true. But really, for our kingdom purposes in the here and now, the people will judge for themselves what is right. In other words, the best people to know how to best follow Jesus and understand their own spirituality are the people engaged in it. Yes, there is a danger here. Things can get off track when the lines of accountability for doctrine and practice become blurry. But the far greater danger is a return to a time when whole cultures were wiped out and suppressed in the name of godliness and civility.

When I worship at Place of Hope, I know it is not my way of following Jesus, but I also know that we are brothers and sisters in Christ. At the same time, I feel unsure and humbled. It is not my "home turf," and I don't quite know how to behave or what is appropriate for a community not my own. I think this is the way it should be. My role there is to listen and learn and perhaps offer something only if I am asked to do so.

I am not there to witness but to be witnessed to. I am there to see and hear about someone else's spiritual journey and life struggle. The people there give of themselves, and we see and hear their vulnerability, and so see and hear from Christ through them.

COME AND SEE IS ABOUT A PERSON, NOT A RELIGION

At the beginning of the gospel of John, Jesus is identified by John the baptist as "the Lamb of God who takes away the sin of the world." Two of John's followers start following Jesus. They literally follow Jesus around. Eventually, Jesus turns to them and asks, "What are you looking for?" They respond by asking where Jesus is staying.

Jesus doesn't respond with theology or religion. He doesn't explain to them who he really is or what his mission is about. That will all come later. All Jesus says to their question of "Where are you staying?" is "Come and see."

The next day, Jesus invites a man named Philip to follow him. Philip goes and finds his friend, Nathanael, and says, "We have found him about whom Moses in the law and also the prophets wrote, Jesus son of Joseph from Nazareth."

Nathanael responds: "Can anything good come out of Nazareth?" How does Philip reply? "Come and see."

The answer of "come and see" is never about getting our beliefs completely right. It is not about religion, or doctrine, or church, or anything like that. It isn't even about a relationship yet. It is simply about curiosity. The first few disciples just followed because they wanted to be with Jesus, though they likely didn't know the fullness of what that meant. Nathanael was curious, and skeptical, and prejudiced ("Can anything good come out of Nazareth?"), but he still went and saw.

Sometimes when we begin pointing people to Jesus, we severely misplace our expectations. We place our own cultural norms and biases upon the person. The Christian church has been doing this for centuries. It continues today, and it must stop. Even Christians who laud their own efforts in cultural relevancy usually have a specific version of Christianity to which they intend to point people.

"Everyone is welcome" is the rallying cry of most churches, yet even those churches that do welcoming exceptionally well often look very homogenous. We have culturally relevant, middle class churches with great music, awesome coffee, where parents feel safe about sending their kids to the beautiful Sunday School programs (except it's called the Kidzone or something even cooler!). It's not that there is anything inherently wrong with these churches; it's that our particular ways of "doing church" tend to shape how we think about "come and see." We often tend to have a certain brand, program, theology, politics, or morality in mind when we are asking people to "come and see," but the original "come and see" was simply about Jesus.

We must recognize that when people of other cultures, spiritualities, philosophies, and political persuasions connect to Jesus and begin following him, it will look very different than our own version of Christianity.

We must not lose sight of the person of Jesus in all of our religion. When examining a culture other than our own, I don't think it is helpful to try and find a parallel to Jesus and just declare "see, we're basically the same." We are not basically the same. Each culture is different, and Jesus is unique. Following Jesus includes allowing Jesus and the Holy Spirit to affirm or deny aspects of culture. As Jesus's sent-ones, we are not the best ones to confront someone else's culture. Instead, we let Jesus and the Spirit do that, not just for other cultures, but for our own as well —especially for our own.

Our primary tasks in disciple-making are listening and loving. We listen to understand, and we offer unconditional love in Christ's name. This, more than anything, will help people see who Jesus really is. If we go to "the nations" with fire and brimstone sermons, telling them about sin and the need to repent, we will have taught that Jesus's primary way of looking at human beings is in judgement, rather than allowing the love of Jesus to shine through.

GO...AND THEN

It is common to have trouble making a move or taking a step. We balk at going outside of our comfort zones, but if you follow Jesus, you won't be following for too long before there is some kind of prompting that sends you beyond your regular patterns or routines.

Each believer needs to develop the ability to listen to God. This is the practice of discernment. How can I know what God is calling me to do or where God is calling me to go? We are used to this way of framing the question, but often have few resources for pursuing an answer.

Discernment can be complicated (especially with respect to big life decisions), but we do have tools at our disposal to help us hear from God more clearly. I have found that a variety of spiritual practices are helpful, including: reading the Scriptures, praying the Examen (see Jim Manney's short but excellent book *A Simple Life-Changing Prayer: Discovering the Power of St. Ignatius Loyola's Examen*), prayer walking, centering prayer (Visit silenceteaches.com for all kinds of information on this), and having a community to check in with and test ideas (this might include family, friends, a church group, a spiritual director, a therapist, a life-coach).

Discernment is ongoing. It is not as if you hear "go"

from God once and then you carry out his single command for the rest of your life. There will be many "gos," and most discernment happens along the way.

This is why this book has been focused on the sending that God does rather than on our discernment that we do prior to going. God commissions us, asking us to take a step, to follow, to go out. Discernment is needed, but we must not endlessly listen before making a move.

You are called to go and so, I encourage you to go.

Go with listening ears and a listening heart - not just listening to God, but to the people to whom you are sent. Be a witness, but more importantly allow yourself to be witnessed to, especially by those different from yourself.

In your witness to Jesus, sort out what is your own cultural and religious baggage, and what it looks like to truly point someone to the love of Jesus. Honestly tell your own story at the right time, and don't downplay it. Your story of God at work in your life is powerful.

Receive the power of the Holy Spirit in your "going," but remember the power and authority you have been given look like the power that Jesus wielded in washing people's feet, touching the unclean, and ultimately laying down his life (and don't forget his harshest judgment was never for "sinners," but for the religious elites).

Pointing people to Jesus ought to always look like love, healing, and grace. If it doesn't, then something is terribly wrong. Allow the Spirit to move you to repent, and begin again in the grace of God.

Go. Take steps. Be directed by the Spirit of God. Then point to Jesus and his love.

QUESTIONS FOR REFLECTION OR DISCUSSION

1) Recall your own story of the Risen Jesus in your life that you developed in the last question of the previous chapter. With fresh eyes, is your story both loving and bold?

2) Who might be witnessing to you in your life? Who do you think God might be placing in your life to strengthen, challenge, or stretch you?

3) How can you point people to Jesus with a "come and see" approach, letting go of your expectations of what following Jesus will look like for someone who is different than you?

4) What do you think your next step is?

RESOURCES FOR CONNECTING WITH GOD

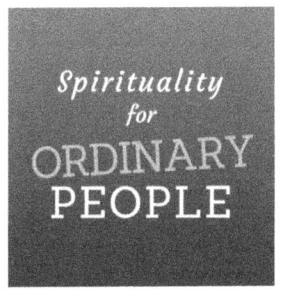

In 2017 I started the Spirituality Ordinary People Website and Podcast to host conversations and provide tips around the broad subject of connecting with God. You can find audio interviews with authors, pastors, artists and other ordinary folk, as well as blog posts, and helpful resources for your own spirituality.

Visit SpiritualityForOrdinaryPeople.com

THANK YOU

It means so much to me that you have taken the time to read *Let God Send*. If you found it helpful, please consider helping to spread the word about this book by doing one the following:

- Leave a rating and review on Amazon - This really helps books get seen by other readers, and means a ton to me as an author - I really do notice it and appreciate the support!
- Tell someone about it, or buy it for someone. You can tell someone on social media, by email, or just in person.
- Email me at matt@mattbrough.com and let me know what you think. I really love hearing from readers.

OTHER "LET GOD" BOOKS

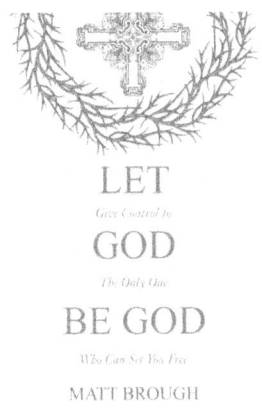

When our desires and God's will don't match up, we often choose to move God from the center of our life to just being an "important part" of it. This book will challenge you to think differently about what it means to have faith. It asks you to set yourself aside, make God your true focus, and trust God to truly be God in your life.

What does it really mean to connect with God? We search for meaning, connection, or guidance, but rarely let go of our pre-conceived notions of what we want to hear. This book asks you to trust God to be present and speak on His terms, rather than insisting that God fit in with your own idea of what He should be doing in your life.

ACKNOWLEDGMENTS

I'd like to thank the congregation of Prairie Presbyterian Church. This group of God's people continues to support me in so many ways, allowing me to pursue creative pursuits like podcasting and writing. My home congregation also provides the occasion for regular preaching and this, more than anything, allows me to try out ideas and explore the Scriptures. All three "Let God" books began as a collection of sermons, so without the preaching habit, they likely never would have been written.

Lauren Craft continues to be an excellent editor, and she is perhaps the most responsible for this book seeing the light of day. I first submitted the manuscript prior to the editing of *Let God Be Present* in 2017 and Lauren helped me to realize that much more work was needed. And by "more work" I mean, I need to start over. *Let God Send* was intended to be the second book in the "Let God" series, but I am so glad it ended up being the final installment. In so many ways, sending is the more urgent theme for me, and now it has worked out that this is a much better, and I think far more helpful, book.

As usual, I had great help from early readers. Thank you to Mary and Sheila for their invaluable proofreading. I am very grateful to Margaret Mullin for reading through the sections on Place of Hope Indigenous Presbyterian Church to ensure that what I was writing was accurate to the practice of that congregation. Thank you as well to J. Dana Trent for agreeing to write the foreword for this book. I am so glad we met a few years ago and have gotten to know one another through podcasts and conversations over the last little while.

With this book, I organized a pre-release book club and got to sit in on a couple of conversations with various groups that used a pre-release version as a book study. These occasions were very helpful and led to a few changes in the final version. Thanks to the Young Adult Group at Prairie Church for making helpful suggestions for the questions in the opening chapters, and thank you to everyone who participated in the online book club.

A big thank you to my wife, Cheryl, for continuing to stand by me in this work, doing far more than provide moral support. She is the co-owner of Thicket Books with me, and we work together to try to put books into the world that we think people will enjoy and will find helpful.

Matt Brough, July 2020

ABOUT THE AUTHOR

Matt Brough has been a pastor of small, faithful congregations for over 15 years. He has served as the director of Cyclical PCC, a Church Planting support initiative of the Presbyterian Church in Canada, and has hosted the Spirituality for Ordinary People Podcast. Matthew is the author of *Let God Be God*, *Let God Be Present*, and also a series of fantasy adventure books for ages eight and up. He lives in Winnipeg, Manitoba, with his wife, Cheryl, and their daughter, Juliet.

You can find out more or be in touch with Matt at his website, mattbrough.com.

www.ingramcontent.com/pod-product-compliance
Lightning Source LLC
Chambersburg PA
CBHW070910080526
44589CB00013B/1244